BEYOND
THE LONELY HEART

What is Love but a wound that bleeds…

And heals, then bleeds again?

The scar remains – sometimes hidden, always hurting,

To others, apparently mended.

A constant reminder of who we are – or once we had.

Never ending. Eternal.

Fátima Ananda Spínola de Abreu

Beyond The Lonely Heart

Spiderwize
Remus House
Coltsfoot Drive
Woodston
Peterborough
PE2 9BF

www.spiderwize.com

A CIP catalogue record for this book is available from the British Library.

The views expressed in this work are solely those of the author and do not necessarily reflect
the views of the publisher, and the publisher hereby disclaims any responsibility for them.

ISBN: 978-1-912694-09-9

BEYOND
THE LONELY HEART

Memoirs of a young immigrant in the 60's

My Mother's story

Fátima Ananda Spínola de Abreu

I held her hand in mine and whispered,

"Thank you mum – for all you have been to me.
You can go - go to God.
I will always, always love you."

This book is for my Mum; my Everything.

Maria Bernardete de Freitas Spínola Paul

RIP

This is my mother's story. And therefore, also mine.

Mine – because she has been my conscience,
my hope and my inspiration;
making me who I am and who I always will be.

In writing this book, I have been true to her words;
those she told me and those she wrote down.

And in doing so, I fulfil my promise to her that I would.

For you my darling mum, my first love –
from my beginning to your end.

Souls joined in love forever.

A Sad Farewell...

Madeira was shrinking. From where she stood, the spire of the city's Cathedral seemed to tremble in sympathy with her own body, and with tears now distorting her vision, she struggled to fix the image to her memory. The mountains beyond were now just shades of grey - as if a cloak of sorrow had been cast over them, all colour removed, and she wondered if her beloved brothers and sisters still stood, straining their eyes as they gazed at the departing ship.

Crying - as she was.

Her home, the tiny island which held all her memories, both good and bad and more than that - the ones she loved so much - was now becoming just a series of indistinguishable shapes, an illusion disappearing before her eyes, as the waves rose and fell.

For a moment she wondered if it would ever become real again. Would she ever return – and if she did, would it be too late?

And in that moment, she felt *so* alone.

It was 23rd September 1964. Bernardete was the one who had to leave – she knew there was no other way. At twenty-five years old, she was saying goodbye to her home, her family - and everything she loved - to travel thousands of miles to a country she knew little about.

In some ways, she was glad it would be her. *She* would be the one to bring hope of a better life to those she cherished - and she was willing to make that sacrifice. Praying that God would give her the courage she needed to face the unknown without them by her side, Bernardete put on a brave face, so that her family would not see, how scared she really was.

Now, carrying just a small orange case which contained her documents and a few items of clothing, she stopped and looked at her mother. It was barely 6am and the sun had not yet risen – but there she was, already bent over the outside sink, arms plunged in freezing water - scrubbing other people's sheets. Her darling grandmother, Arsénia, rosary in hand as always – sat at the small table, silent tears running down her cheeks.

Bernardete's heart was heavy with sadness as she observed her mother's hunched shoulders and greying hair, tied as always into a neat bun at the nape of her neck. She whispered,

"It's time Mãe"…

Without turning, Maria replied,

"God go with you my daughter," and Bernardete embraced her grandmother, unlatched the gate, and left her home – her mother's sobs now echoing with her own.

A Time, Before...

The events of recent years had left Bernardete's family struggling with poverty. Her father, Julio had been ill for a while and it had become harder for him to work the land which provided the sustenance that they needed to survive.

Bernardete was just seven years old when her parents made the difficult decision to relocate to another village, with hope of better opportunities there. Eventually, they decided upon an area previously known to Julio - situated roughly ten miles north of their hometown. The village had its own doctor – and it was clear that Julio's health would need regular monitoring.

For Maria and Julio, leaving their extended family was heart-breaking - to the children however, it was an adventure. Excitedly they said goodbye to their grandparents, aunts, uncles and cousins and set off to follow their parents as they began the perilous journey ahead.

Within just a few hours, excitement had changed to groans of exhaustion as their little feet, barely protected in shabby shoes, began to ache and sting. Encouraging them onwards, Maria and Julio took turns to carry the littlest ones, whilst struggling to pull a makeshift cart which held their few belongings. It was not easy, the rough, hilly terrain added both time and effort to the crossing.

Bernardete was just glad to have her own shoes. Like most of the children in their village, she was usually barefoot – between them, the sisters had just one pair which they had to share. These shoes, always pristinely polished and immaculately clean, were only used on Sundays for going to church.

Because they only had the one pair, they had to take turns to attend the service. The oldest would go first and then hurry home to her sister who was waiting impatiently and ready to pull the shoes right out of her hands. The sight was common – many of the village children had the same routine and would panic as the priest stood at the door - scolding and hurrying them along. As luck would have it, the sisters had the same sized feet, and would have – for their entire lives!

Despite all this, the extreme poverty and sometimes their empty bellies, the children were happy - naïve to the problems having no money can bring.

Exhausted, the family finally reached Santana, a rural village north east of the Island. Well populated valleys were overlooked by the Laurisilva forest, its intoxicating scent wafting down from the mountains to create a fresh clean air for the residents who lived below.

The houses typical to that area were unusual but quaint, triangular in shape with two rooms and a loft which was mainly used for storage. Julio moved his family into one of these – the children slept in the attic and he and his wife had one of the rooms downstairs.

Much of the surrounding land was farmland and used for agriculture. Chickens wandered freely and those farmers who were financially more affluent, would sometimes own a goat or a pig. These animals were a useful commodity to those who could afford them as they could be sold on for a profit.

7

If a family was resourceful, they would buy a share of the animal, including the costs of raising them. At Christmas, it would be slaughtered and the meat shared out accordingly.

It was not unusual for Bernardete to come across a neighbour seated with a dead pig's head in her lap, burning the hairs off its face. The little girl would rush past - trying to avert her eyes, as its own stared blankly at her.

It smelt good cooking though!

Madeira was a place of festivals. Every town and village had its own patron saint and recognised its feast-day with a procession leading from the church. There always seemed to be an excuse to celebrate with parties in the surrounding streets. If it wasn't for a saint, it would be an onion festival, a wine festival – anything that would add to the collection plate of the parish.

The poorest of all would give what little they had to the priest, assured by him that their souls would be blessed for the gift they had given. It was not unusual for the statues in the church to be laden with gold chains – family heirlooms passed from one generation to the next – whilst its people went hungry.

All the children delighted in the religious festivals and Bernardete in particular loved to watch the procession. Solemnly she would stand, palms pressed together as it passed her by – the image of whichever particular saint being celebrated held high and carried by the most pious members of the church. Little girls, dressed in white would lead the way singing songs of praise and Bernardete would watch them in envy – wishing that she herself, was one of them - pure and, resembling an angel.

Sometimes, when a festival was imminent, their father would try and put aside a coin or two and surprise them with sweets from one of the stalls which lined the main street.

The girls' favourite was a foil string in bright colours – red, gold, green or blue – twisted at intervals with each twist hiding an individual sugary treat. They would stroll around for days wearing these proudly as a necklace until they could no longer resist the temptation to eat what was inside. By now, the sweets were just a sticky mess, stuck solidly to their wrappers but - undeterred, the sisters would lick the string until they could see right through the coloured foils.

Occasionally, Julio would bring them a baked dough doll (*boneca de massa*) – these were simple pastries made of flour, water and yeast with seeds for eyes and coloured

9

ribbons for the hair and clothes. The girls enjoyed playing with them more than eating them. They had a very odd taste.

Sometimes, Julio would take his two eldest sons and they would be gone for days, travelling from one village to another to harvest the grapes which were ripe - and ready to be made into wine. It was an intensely labouring job – usually taking place once a year in September. Exhausted, they would eventually return, with their shoulders bruised from carrying the heavy baskets – and feet stained purple, from treading the fruit.

The women too, did what they could to contribute to the family's finances. They would traditionally be expected to do handiwork to sell, either crotchet, tapestry or embroidery - and Santana was renowned for its talented women workers.

Already skilled in needlework, Maria would collect the raw material and prepare it for the time-consuming task ahead. As a mother, her role included training her own daughters in these ways of old and so, she gathered them around her to help - as soon as they were able to follow instruction.

The little girls would huddle together, seated on the warm ground beside their mother, watching and learning as - with blistered fingers from the needle, she taught them to

10

sew. In front of her she had laid out a large linen cloth, already marked with intricate designs printed in blue indigo ink. The ink had a pungent stink - similar to paraffin, which Bernardete hated. It gave her headaches and made her feel sick. She knew she would not do this job when she grew up – she couldn't stand it!

Over time, the girls would each clutch their own corner of the fabric and very carefully embroider over the exquisite pattern, using a variety of stitches for each different section. Once complete, these would be sent on to the embroidery factory in the city - to be cut, washed and pressed. At last – finished and ready to sell, these beautiful pieces were then distributed amongst the tourist shops which lined the city's seafront. Visitors to the island would seek out the most detailed handmade tablecloths, willing to pay extortionate amounts in recognition of the expert handiwork involved.

For this eye-straining work, Maria, just as many of the other women on the island, received a pittance. Although she was well aware of the real value of her labour, she was still grateful for anything that would help feed her family.

At times, Maria's brother would visit them on the way back from delivering produce from his farm, to neighbouring villages. He had – in the time since they'd left, bought a small pickup truck and all the children would gather around the vehicle begging to be lifted up. Dutifully, he would pick up his nieces and nephews one by one – where they would wave down to the other children as they stood looking on in envy.

Their uncle never arrived empty handed and for a while after his visit, they would have plenty of vegetables, enjoying nutritious soups prepared by their mother. Sometimes, Julio would return with him, back to his home town of Machico, to help out on the farm before coming home to his wife with a little extra money.

It was the way of life. Each of them – from child to adult – did whatever necessary to make a living.

The family remained in Santana for several years and, for a while, Julio seemed quite well. Maria was happy – she loved the pretty village and the little house which, although tiny, was warm and comfortable. Wild flowers surrounded the home - including hydrangeas in blues and pinks, orchids of every shape and colour and many other beautiful plants - cultivated by God Himself.

During their time there, the couple had another two children, a girl and then another boy. However, within a

12

couple of years of the birth of their son, Julio started to complain of pains in his stomach and found himself, once again, unable to work.

Maria realised that - if he was to ever get well, they would need a proper diagnosis of his illness and access to the correct medication. Even perhaps, a hospital.

For the second time, they gathered their children together, packed up their belongings and began the long journey to the island's capital, Funchal.

People had advised them that the warmer climate, further south, would probably help to improve Julio's health. With the help of relatives who already lived there, they had managed to find a place to stay whilst they looked for something more permanent. Before too long, they found a house to rent, located just above the city's centre.

Their new home overlooked the bay and was positioned just above the city. It was small – too small for the ten people living within but Maria hoped that the change would improve things for her husband.

Sadly, it did little to change his outlook and so, burdened with the costs for medical examinations and medication, Maria had reluctantly made her older children abandon their education – she simply could not pay for their schooling any more. They willingly did this and tried to find employment where they could.

Getting up in the middle of the night, the two older boys would walk down the hundreds of steps into the town centre to unpack fruit and vegetables for the market stallholders, before their customers started to arrive from dawn. The girls in turn, did whatever possible to contribute towards the family's needs - even the youngest took up the cooking so that their mother could dedicate her time to taking care of their sick father. As his illness progressed, much of their earnings was surrendered in order to pay for him to travel to Lisbon for treatment.

Sadly, it had been in vain and he had died in his early fifties, leaving his wife with young children - and a broken heart.

At fifty-seven years old, a widow, with the youngest child just six, Maria accepted all the work she could find. She washed, cleaned and ironed for strangers – often with tears of grief rolling down her face.

Her own father had died the very same year and Maria felt such intense sorrow at having lost the two men she loved the most. However, there was no time for mourning or for self-pity – she simply continued, trying to hide her pain, aware that her family relied on her strength. Now, with her elderly mother to take care of too, she was fearful that they would become destitute.

The intention had been for the whole family to travel to Brazil, in the footsteps of Julio's brothers and sister who had left Madeira some years previous, in the hope that their lives would be improved. His oldest son, João, had emigrated in 1957 and had written, assuring his father of better prospects in South America. Sadly, as soon as he left, the dream of being reunited disappeared as all savings were spent on medicines in an attempt to cure Julio's illness.

Bernardete recalled her oldest brother's face. She had loved him dearly and had missed him so much since he'd left them. That day, he had been so excited - there had been no sadness as they had all anticipated joining him eventually. João had borrowed the money for his trip and had waved goodbye, intending to return with enough money to pay for his family's passages - or at least, to help his mother and those he had left behind.

That was the last time any of them saw him.

Bernardete, her eyes now searching for a sign of the place she had just left, thought about the last few years. She remembered a time when, with just a loaf of bread between ten people, her mother had shared out a meal, pretending to chew a piece herself. But she had noticed... her beloved mother had none.

She remembered the cornmeal porridge (milho), mixed with a little chopped cabbage – 'poor man's food' which had sustained them many times.

She pictured herself feeding her father as he lay shivering on the old straw mattress, struggling with pain... She barely remembered him out of that bed. He had suffered so much but rarely complained, greeting each of his children with a gentle smile despite his agony. How she missed that smile.

At night, Bernardete would often lay awake, aware of her mother's sobbing. Gently rising, she and her sisters would quietly go outside to find her sitting in the dark, alone and staring out to sea. The Atlantic Ocean with shimmering specks of light from the fishing boats, glistening like fireflies in the distance. Silently they stood beside her, helpless as together, they listened to their father's pitiful groans from inside the bedroom. They knew he was trying his best to suppress them... but still the sounds escaped.

Bernardete recalled members of their extended family, those who had done their best to help them as things got worse. The uncle who turned up at their gate breathless, having travelled for many miles - much of it by foot - carrying a sack of potatoes on his shoulder and a bag of beans inside his jacket.

The aunt who had visited their father every time he was in hospital and afterwards, climbing the winding narrow alleyways past her own home – to bring the poor family a loaf of bread and a few vegetables.

Meat was a rarity in their house. The cost was beyond Maria – and on the rare occasion that they had a little pork, it was immediately prepared for Bernardete's father in the hope that he would regain some strength.

She remembered on one occasion, her mother had made a thin broth with beans. Bernardete had acquired a habit of pushing her beans to the edge of her plate so that she could savour them at the end... when she noticed one of them sprouting legs and scrambling over the side! It was a cockroach! She had lost her appetite that day!

This memory brought a smile to her face as she recalled how it had made her sisters laugh till they cried!

There had been good times too – before. As children, they had not really been aware of the lack of money – sure, they were hungry, but wasn't everyone?

With so many siblings, there was always laughter and always someone willing to play. They had no toys but there was plenty of land on which they were able to run around after each other, playing amongst the colourful flowers which grew so naturally outside their home.

Bernardete's eldest brother had always been very inventive and, using whatever resource he could find, he would sometimes make his younger siblings things to play with. Just by bending a piece of rubber into a circle and tying a rope around the waists of each little one, he made them a bus! Bernardete remembered the arguments as each one pleaded to be at the front, grabbing the rubber 'steering wheel' so that they could be the bus driver.

As she stood alone on the deck reminiscing on those days and the struggles the family had endured, Bernardete made a silent promise that - while God gave her strength, she would send *every* spare penny back home.

18

A Journey Taken...

Turning from the surrounding waters, Bernardete picked up her case and headed inside to the Boarding lounge. Showing her ticket, she was welcomed and given details of how to get to her cabin. On one of the walls was a large map of the ship and she noted that her own accommodation was located on one of the lower floors. It was all so overwhelming.

The air was thick with excitement as people swarmed all around her. Big suitcases blocked her path and small children got in her way as their parents struggled to hold onto them, worried they might be caught up in the crowd and lost.

Bernardete struggled to get through the crowd and stood for a moment against the wall, to catch her breath.

Looking around, she noticed a family who she recognised from the docks in Funchal. She had heard them mention that they were travelling within the same class as her, so she quickly made her way over to stand beside them and said hello. Realising then, that they were situated on the same floor, she followed them down a huge staircase and into a large foyer.

The group paused for a moment to admire the hall. Glistening mahogany panels adorned every wall and above them, twinkling chandeliers hung down from the high ceilings, ornately decorated with patterns of gold. Large vases of tropical flowers stood in the corners and every table held exquisite floral arrangements in the centre.

All around them, groups of passengers were sitting, excitedly chatting in loud voices. Others were standing, confused, as they tried to decipher which direction to take.

Bernardete suddenly remembered the group she was following and began to panic, realising that they had moved away from her side. Wildly, she looked around and was relieved to spot them in the near distance. She rushed to catch them up, running past the bustling porters as they pushed trolleys, laden with suitcases and bursting at the seams.

Exhausted, she stood beside the small group and slipped discreetly behind them as they waited for the lift.

It finally came to a halt on the level where her room was situated and Bernardete, following the family in front, stepped out into another hallway.

She looked around. Long corridors headed off in every direction and soon, so did the other passengers. Feeling anxious, Bernardete wondered which way to go and prayed that she would not get lost. She suddenly noticed that there were arrows on the walls, indicating the direction to each set of cabins in numerical order. It was at that point that she realised just how enormous the ship was - the numbers went into hundreds!

Passing door after door, she looked carefully at the numbers on each one until at last, she reached her own. Taking out her key, she slowly turned it in the lock and stepped inside.

There were two beds and Bernardete guessed that she would be sharing with a stranger for the forthcoming days. The room was exquisite in her eyes – far removed from the one she had at home.

There had been a time when she had shared one bed with her three sisters and she recalled the excitement they had felt, when the first had left to marry. Although they had missed her being at home - oh the bliss of more space! She knew that her youngest sister, now the only girl at home, would be over the moon to have the bed to herself!

Sitting down on one of the beds, she opened up her case and examined the items she had carefully packed within. Lifting out her clothes, she hung them up neatly in the single wardrobe next to the bed she had chosen for herself. As she straightened out the pleated skirts and pretty blouses, she felt pleased that she at least had a few nice things to wear. From what she had seen of the other passengers, there was a certain dress code expected – even for those travelling as she was, in the cheaper immigrants' accommodation.

Bernardete had received training as a seamstress and right up until just a few days before her voyage, had been working as tailor for the police force, making their uniforms. She had managed to save a little money and in her spare time, had selected a quantity of budget fabrics and made a few outfits to take with her on her journey.

Over the last few months, she had studiously watched the tourists who visited the island as they explored the streets around her place of work - memorising the cut and style of their clothes. The English ladies, with their heels and smart tight skirts often struggled to walk the cobbled narrow streets, but in Bernardete's fascinated eyes, still managed to look so elegant. She was determined to try and copy the styles popular in England which, although similar were more refined than she was used to in Madeira. Her mother had been shocked at the length of the skirts she had made, but had kept quiet, not wanting her girl to be isolated in her new environment and instead, trusted her judgement to God's Holy will.

A devout Catholic, Bernardete smiled as she picked up her treasured little plastic triptych which contained within, an icon of our Lady of Fátima together with the three little shepherds which she had appeared to in Portugal. Maria had insisted she take it with her and she was now grateful for the comfort of something from home. Bringing it close to her lips, she kissed the Virgin's head as she said a silent prayer for her mother.

Her older brother, as she was leaving, had pinned a golden brooch onto the lapel of her jacket – it was beautiful with a red jewel in the centre. He had hugged her with tears in his eyes as he told her to remember him whenever she looked at this small token of his love. It had taken all of her strength not to take his arm and return back home. Just two years older than her, he had always been her chaperone, accompanying her whenever she journeyed into the city - and was a constant friend as well as devoted brother. She carefully removed the brooch and placed it inside her purse for safekeeping – not really knowing whether it was valuable - but knowing that she would treasure it always for the depth of love within the gift.

Bernardete suddenly remembered something else. As they stood at the quayside, her older sister, heavily pregnant and distraught at her departure, had discreetly put a little wrapped package into her hand. Embracing her tightly, she had made Bernardete promise to keep it with her for as long as she lived.

She had kissed her goodbye, heartbroken that she would not be there when the baby was born and said to her,

"Name her Fátima – if it's a girl. After our Lady."

Finding the parcel now, Bernardete carefully unwrapped it. Inside was a small blue metal crucifix, the image of Jesus in silver. Again, with a kiss, she carefully placed it on the little table next to her bed.

She returned to unpacking the rest of her case and suddenly noticed the corner of an envelope in amongst the rest of her things. Her breath stopped as she pulled out two small photographs. Tears began to flow once again as she looked down at the pictures of her mother and father.

"Hello!"

Bernardete turned to see a young woman struggling with a suitcase in the doorway. "Looks like we're sharing!" the girl said, cheerfully.

Welcoming the distraction, Bernardete wiped her eyes and, forcing away thoughts of sadness, she quickly got up to help.

Within the next few hours, they had shared details of their families, homes and dreams and a feeling of hope started to rise within her. It was a start - she had made a new friend.

Now, with a companion, Bernardete felt more at ease and began to look forward to the next few days. Together, the girls gave each other the confidence to explore and to enjoy everything on offer during the journey.

The ship was called the Queen Mary and would take them directly to Southampton, England. Both women were overwhelmed by its size and magnitude - and excited at the prospect of things available for them to enjoy in the five days before they reached their destination.

Together, they explored each hall, marvelling as they walked through the many lavish dining rooms and stopping to admire the exquisite paintings on each wall. There were some areas of the ship that were not accessible and restricted for first class passengers only. The girls were curious but really did not mind – there was certainly enough for them to see and do elsewhere.

Each night, there was a variety of entertainment available for them to enjoy. The girls eagerly made the most of every experience, using the facilities on offer and eating food they had never dreamed of tasting. They were first up to dance at every evening reception and first in line for the theatrical shows each afternoon.

Bernardete was shocked at the abundance of food ready for consumption at any time - day or night. At mealtimes, buffet tables heaved with every type of meat, fish, cakes, every possible taste and appetite was catered for - and more! Deserts were piled high with fresh cream and fruit, some of which she had never even seen before. Bernardete savoured every taste, wishing that her mother could be with her to eat the delicacies denied to her for lack of money. She felt almost guilty as she tried the tasty dishes – and felt sad to see how much was discarded on the plates of those who had filled them higher than they could possibly eat.

Bernardete made a vow to herself that she would work really hard so that one day, her mother would be able to enjoy meat at every meal - if she so wished.

There were many other young people on board and sharing the experience brought many of them together. Bernardete soon realised that many of the young women especially, were just like her - and emigrating for a chance to help their own families back home in Madeira. They all had jobs waiting for them in England – as trainee nurses, housemaids and au-pairs.

At that time, emigrants had to have a guarantee of occupation, residence and a responsible sponsor, before they could leave their country to go somewhere new. In Madeira, agencies were set up to match sponsors with those wishing to travel to England. A fee would be paid to the agency and the sponsor in turn, would receive a sum of money to assume

27

responsibility for the individual. For that, they would have to arrange a job and accommodation and ensure that they adhered to the law and regulations attached to their work permits.

The business was totally legit, and the only option for those who had no contacts of their own in the country they wished to work in. It was an easy – if slightly risky way for the sponsor to receive a guaranteed some of money. With regards to those leaving Madeira, most of their sponsors were Portuguese women who, keen to make a bit of extra money had already been through the process themselves and had earned a right to stay in their adopted country.

Many of the young women on the journey had this in common and so spent much of their time together. They vowed to meet up once they were all settled in England, not realising that a reunion was actually highly unlikely due to the distance between them and work pressures. For those five days together at least, they could dream and plan…

It was an amazing experience and Bernardete, pleased to have made new friends, loved everything about the trip and dreamed that maybe, this might be the kind of career for her – on a ship, travelling the world.

All too soon, the journey was ending and, like the other passengers, Bernardete found herself up on the deck. She gazed out at a grey coastline overlooked by an even greyer sky.

She was beginning to feel slightly apprehensive as she looked down at the docks. She saw many hands waving excitedly to greet their loved ones. How she wished there was someone waiting there for her…

Picking up her case, she followed the group towards the steps and hugged the friends she had made on the journey, each of them promising to stay in touch. Ahead of her she could see a line of people, their expressions a mixture of excitement and nerves as they headed in the direction of Immigration control. Bernardete was trembling as she reached the front of the queue and shaking, took her papers out of her handbag to hand to the official sitting at the desk.

He looked down at her documents for what seemed like an eternity…

"I'm sorry Miss, but your work permit has expired. I'm afraid you will have to go back to Portugal!" Bernardete thought she had misunderstood, her English was not so good and she looked at him blankly. He pointed to the boat and showed her the date on the document. It then dawned on her that, in the time it took for her to contemplate and convince herself that leaving her homeland was her only option, the six months had somehow expired!

Bernardete was overwhelmed and so afraid! Shaking visibly, she took the hands of the uniformed officer and begged him, "Please, please, no! I borrowed money to come – I can't pay back if you send me home! My family – no money!" By now she was sobbing uncontrollably and the officer felt sorry for the young girl. Smiling at her kindly, he gently asked her to sit down and wait.

Three hours passed and Bernardete cried endlessly, terrified at what would become of her. All the other girls had left already, glancing back sympathetically when they realised that she was in trouble. Yet not one had stopped to offer support – they all had new destinations to get to. All she could do was pray, begging God to help her as so many different thoughts ran through her mind… how would she pay the loan of her passage? She knew that her family would be pleased to see her but wouldn't they be disappointed once they had realised that her return would leave them worse off than before? On top of this - the shame of being sent back home because of a stupid mistake – people would gossip and laugh and make fun of her... "Oh God, please help me!" It was unbearable...

"Miss?"

She looked up, filled with dread as she saw a policeman standing over her.

"You are lucky," he told her, "Your employer has agreed to renew your work permit for you, and so it has been arranged for me to escort you to meet her at Waterloo Station. She will arrange everything. But the slightest problem Miss – you will have to go back!"

Bernardete was overjoyed! A little embarrassed that she would have a police escort, she was also relieved that she would not be making the journey to London, on her own. She thanked God for coming to her aid. Picking up her case once again, she hurriedly followed the officer towards the station and boarded the train.

This was all new to her. There had not been a train in Madeira for many years and it was the first time Bernardete had ever seen one for real. The policeman indicated that she should sit down and he took his place opposite her.

The journey to Waterloo Station took two hours and, thankfully the policeman did not speak to her at all. Self-conscious of her limited knowledge of English, Bernardete in turn, avoided looking directly at him in case he started a conversation. Instead, she stared out of the window and marvelled at the unfamiliar landscape as the train sped past.

England was very pretty. And flat. Bernardete realised that she would have to get used to a very different environment – there were no mountains here - but perhaps London itself would be more like home, with cobbled streets and surrounded by colourful flowers… She was in for a shock.

They finally pulled into the station and nervously, she glanced up at the policeman. He rewarded her with a kind smile as he stood and lifted her case down from the shelf above her head. Directing her towards the open door, he led her off the train. Bernardete once again asked God for courage as she stepped onto the platform, at the same time, her eyes searching frantically for her Godmother. It was *she* who had originally written to Maria and offered to be Bernardete's sponsor. She had already arranged employment and accommodation for the young woman and had assured her mother that she would be there to meet her.

With a sigh of relief, Bernardete spotted the familiar figure though she had not seen her for several years. Beside

32

her stood a woman, well-dressed and probably in her thirties – Bernardete imagined that this must be her new employer.

The two women had seen her and were now waving in her direction. Pointing them out, she followed the policeman who - satisfied that he had done his duty, handed her over to the women and wished her well. As he left, he turned to Bernardete's Godmother and said, "Make sure that you put her documents in order as soon as possible. Until then, she will have to report to her local police station every week." Assured that this would happen, he said goodbye, leaving the women together to become acquainted.

Once outside the station, they got into a taxi and her Godmother briefly explained her role as au-pair to the family. The other woman smiled at her encouragingly, taking time to ask her about her home and family back in Madeira. She listened patiently as Bernardete attempted to respond to her questions, in broken English. The lady did not sound like the policeman, her accent sounded different. Bernardete soon discovered that this was because she was French. "This will not be easy" she thought.

She was astonished to hear that there were nine children, ranging from the age of just one month to eleven years old. As the au-pair, she would be expected to take care of most of their needs as well as some housework. Bernardete felt a little daunted – it seemed a lot. However, she convinced herself it would be fine – she was after all, used to hard work.

After a short while, the taxi pulled into a side street just off High Street Kensington, a popular area of West London. All around were shops and people rushing along – some of them running to catch the bright red buses which filled the busy roads. It was now starting to become difficult to see at all. There was a thickening fog which seemed to be slowly enveloping everything around her.

Now standing on the pavement, her Godmother kissed her on both cheeks and reminded her to visit on her day off. Bernardete promised and turned to follow her employer up the concrete steps and into her new home.

A Portuguese Saint in London...

The houses were very close together. There were no gardens, just small concrete yards which the residents had clearly tried to brighten with a few colourful pots.

Bernardete recognised some of the plants – but they were nowhere near as vibrant as the multitude of flowers which had surrounded, not only her mother's small house, but the whole island. Visitors had come from all over the world just to see the *floating garden in the Atlantic*. She had often watched them arrive on ships as she looked out from the veranda of her mother's house, which overlooked the bay of Funchal and its port.

Stepping into a wide hallway, Bernardete discreetly assessed her surroundings, admiring the mahogany furniture that glistened brightly with fresh polish.

She compared them to the few faded things they had back home. Shabby as they were, she missed them – her mother and sisters' hand-made embroideries had always made them beautiful.

She became suddenly aware of several little faces, watching her through the banisters of a vast, white staircase. Bernardete smiled as shyly, the children appeared one by one to greet her. Introduced to each of them in turn, she was taken upstairs to see her room and felt instantly comforted, as one of the little girls slipped a hand into hers and led the way.

She looked around. It was small but furnished nicely with a wardrobe, a side-table and a desk - and sink in the corner. The bed was freshly made and a vase of flowers stood on the table by its side.

The children's mother told her to take her time settling in and invited her to come down for dinner - whenever she was ready.

Bernardete's work was to begin at 7am the next morning and so, after the meal - and exhausted from the day's events, she said goodnight and slipped straight into bed. For a while, she lay there, contemplating her journey to this point.

Her eyes began to fill as she gazed over at the little luminous statue of our Lady of Fátima, now glowing next to her in the darkness. As her tears fell, she lay in that strange, unfamiliar room and prayed for guidance.

Before she finally slept, she said a final prayer for her family and herself, so that one day, she might return to them - and her home.

As the days passed by, Bernardete eventually fell into a routine. Each morning, she had to feed the younger children and get the older ones ready for school. During the day, she would wash, iron, clean, make beds and prepare food for their return. The mother helped, but having recently given birth and with the youngest to take care of, she really did not have the energy to do much else.

The husband was hardly ever around as he worked long hours. Doing what – she didn't know.

Bernardete worked very hard and - except for Sundays and some evenings after the children were in bed, she had little time to relax. She felt constantly exhausted and generally fed up.

Sometimes, her boss would send her out on errands and she enjoyed this break in routine, soon becoming familiar with the streets immediately surrounding her own. She would deliberately taking a longer route, enjoying the chance to spend those extra minutes looking in the shop windows and admiring the variety of things displayed.

Many of the shops along the nearby streets sold only furniture. As Bernardete passed, she was surprised to see that they were not new but instead, chipped and faded! They looked almost as worn and shabby as her mother's old furniture back home. But the prices!

She could not believe that people would pay such amounts for old chairs and tables and yet the customers inside, dressed immaculately in expensive clothing – were obviously willing to part with their money for such things. She could not understand it.

Whilst out on one of these errands one afternoon, Bernardete had wandered into a nearby side street, curious to see what lay ahead. Making a mental note of the direction in which she was travelling, so that she could retrace her steps and not get lost, she ventured forward.

Soon, she found herself outside a Catholic Church. Excited at this discovery, Bernardete stepped inside and was surprised to be greeted by a statue of St. Anthony - standing right in the entrance, as if waiting for her.

She felt immediately comforted at the sight of the Portuguese saint and felt in her purse for a coin so that she could light a candle. She looked around the dark church and her eyes were drawn instinctively towards the altar.

On one side, sat upon a gold throne was a beautiful statue of our Lady, holding the child Jesus in her lap. Bernardete paused for a while in front of the image and got down to her knees to ask the Blessed Mother to hold all those she missed, as lovingly as she held her own precious baby.

It was a church that would bring her much comfort in the years ahead, a place of refuge and peace where she could collect her thoughts and gather courage.

Bernardete's favourite shop on Kensington High Street was Barkers. This was a very large department store which sold everything anyone could need – or want!

The store was renowned for its impressive window displays and Bernardete would often stand mesmerised as young girls busied themselves, dressing life-like mannequins in bright buttoned-down jackets and pencil skirts.

Others artistically created 'pretend' living rooms complete with upholstered furnishings and lights... whilst realistic good-looking dummies of gentleman - wearing fine black suits, leaned against ornately decorated fireplaces as they clinked crystal glasses together in mock celebration.

She loved to see the changing displays and was often caught out by one of the dressers – suddenly embarrassed that they had caught her staring!

Occasionally, she was sent to buy groceries from the food department and before collecting these items would spend a while wandering around the store. She never ceased to be amazed at the assortment of things for sale. From food to furniture, hats and clothes to toys, books and stationery – there was no end to the choice available and all inside one shop!

Bernardete particularly loved the haberdashery section and would stroll amongst the fabrics, pausing to feel the delicate materials on display. Coloured silks hung down in every colour; threads and yarns in every shade. She couldn't stop herself from touching the bright ribbons, buttons and lace trimmings, as she paused to admire the varieties available.

Stopping to look through the array of sewing patterns, Bernardete dreamed of owning a sewing machine of her own. On more than one occasion, she was unable to resist the temptation to buy a pattern and would place the little packet carefully in her handbag. She hoped that, one day she would be in a position to create the outfit so delicately printed on the front of each one.

There were sometimes off-cuts of material available at a reduced price and Bernardete would eagerly search through, happy to find something suited to the patterns she had previously bought. These precious items would be collected together and hidden away in the little orange suitcase under her bed - in anticipation of the day that they could be used.

It made her happy to know that she had them and motivated her towards the goal of buying her own sewing machine. Just as soon as she had saved enough...

Bernardete had been overjoyed to discover that the family were, like herself, devout Catholics. Each Sunday, she gladly accompanied them to the Carmelites church – the very same one that she had discovered earlier on. The service was celebrated in Latin, just as it was back home and so she was more or less able to follow, the order of the Mass. Standing with her eyes closed, she imagined that her family was there beside her.

Afterwards, they would all return to the house and she would give the children breakfast and help prepare lunch. Once that was done, she was able to do whatever she wished, Sunday afternoons were her own free time.

Most weeks, she would take a bus to visit her Godmother who lived nearby in Olympia. There was often a strange fog even during the day which made her a bit cautious about being out by herself and so, as the weather got colder and the evenings darker, she resorted to sitting in her room and writing letters home. In a house occupied by so many, Bernardete was very lonely.

As time went by, Bernardete managed to save a little of her salary each week and finally, bought herself the sewing machine she had dreamed of. It sat, pride of place, on the little table in her bedroom – a pastel blue Singer inside its own smart case. Bernardete felt so proud and showed it to her boss – at last she would be able to use the patterns she had been collecting. Among these were a few that she had deliberately picked up for young boys and with her brother in mind, she couldn't wait to get started on some new clothes to send him.

How she missed her little brother... she recalled that, on the day she had left Madeira, her mother had sent him to stay at a friend's house so that he would not see Bernardete leave. Everyone had felt that it would have been too traumatic for him and he would not have understood why she had to go. He was just a little boy. Bernardete had wondered whether it had been the right thing to do – she was afraid that he might hate her for not saying goodbye – or worse, think that *she* didn't care. The truth was, that she would not have been able to walk out of the gate and see him standing there, as unhappy as she was. She loved him so much.

Everyone had said – and she had believed - that it would hurt less this way. It still hurt.

When she had first met the oldest child from this family, it had nearly broken her heart. He was roughly the same age - and skinny too, with the same dark hair and pale skin as her own brother. Every time she looked at him, she remembered that day.

Now with a purpose, Bernardete looked forward to the evenings when she could lose herself in her hobby, carefully ironing the finished outfits she had made before packaging

43

them up to post back home. She was determined that her precious brother should have the opportunities his siblings never did and be able to complete his studies – he should never have to endure the poverty they had.

Her boss had noticed how skilled she was and somehow managed to include additional sewing tasks into Bernardete's job description. She would ask the young woman to alter the children's clothes, letting down hems and adjusting waistbands as well as sewing loose buttons onto her and her husband's own clothing. Bernardete did not mind at first but realised that she was still expected to complete her other chores and so the sewing ended up being done during her own time in the evenings. She also found that she was using her own threads and needles, which she had to keep replacing. It didn't seem fair.

The woman had also seen the shirts and shorts that Bernardete had made which were intended for her brother and she had commented on how professional they looked. Immediately, she asked that Bernardete make new dresses for each of her six daughters – promising to buy the fabric and to compensate her for her time. Eagerly, the young woman agreed – hopefully it would relieve her of some of the housework and the extra money would definitely be welcome.

However, to Bernardete's disappointment, this too was just incorporated into the work expected of her, and she received no extra financial reward at all.

She was hurt but too shy to complain. She knew that she was being taken advantage of, but what could she do?

She had fallen in love with the family and the children adored her – but she realised then that she could never progress any further if she remained in the job. Something would have to change, and soon.

Bernardete was struggling to manage on the low wages. Although the family did not charge her for rent or food, she had to buy her own toiletries and warm clothes. In addition, she had to find money to send home *and* pay back what she still owed for her trip. Of course she also wanted to keep up with the fashions of London, but unable to afford much, continued to make her own clothes instead. However, there were some things that she couldn't make – or do without.

A warm coat, jumpers – she had not brought any of these from home, having never experienced cold enough to need them.

Out of her small wage, she tried to set aside a little bit every week as savings and she would send the same amount home to her mother. It didn't seem very much and she hoped that her family understood her situation. What else could she do? She never really treated herself – the sewing machine had been to help them too - and was her one and only indulgence.

It couldn't go on this way and each night, Bernardete prayed for a solution to her troubles.

A Chance Encounter...

One Sunday afternoon, Bernardete was strolling along Oxford Street and she suddenly heard a familiar voice, shouting out in Portuguese…

"Bernardete! Oh my God – what are you doing in London?" It was Isabel, an old friend from back home! Laughing, they hugged each other, both trying to speak at the same time. There was a café nearby and so excitedly linking arms, they went inside to catch up on each other's news.

On hearing how much work she had to do - and how unfairly she was being paid, Isabel felt very sad for her friend and offered to try and find her a job.

She had been working for University College Hospital since her own arrival in the country.

"You would love it there Bernardete! I've made so many friends and we go out a lot together in the evenings! Let me try and arrange an interview for you. Wouldn't it be great if we could work together?" Excited, she went on and on about how fantastic it was – Bernardete agreed that it sounded perfect for her.

She was surprised to hear how much Isabel earned – she had more money and more time off with much less responsibility. In addition, the staff were each allocated a room in the staff hostel which cost them very little in rent.

Agreeing to let her friend put her name forward, Bernardete returned to the house with new hope.

The next morning, Isabel called to say that she had spoken to her manager and she had agreed to interview Bernardete at 3pm, the following day!

She was so excited – Our Lady of Fátima was really watching over her and she felt confident she would be offered a job.

Just to be sure, she spent most of the night praying.

Isabel met her in Oxford Circus and together, they took the short walk to Gower Street. The manager seemed very nice and asked just a few questions before immediately offering her a job, serving food in the Doctor's canteen. Bernardete was overjoyed although she felt slightly down-hearted at the realisation that it would be sad to leave the children. She had grown to love each of them.

That evening, she told the family of her decision. The mother begged her to reconsider, assuring her that she would increase her salary and also promising to give her another afternoon off.

The reaction of the children was something she hadn't expected. The little ones had flung themselves at her, sobbing uncontrollably at this devastating news. Crying too, she hugged them, but she could not go back on her decision. She promised to return and visit whenever she could.

She was very sad, but knew in her heart that it was the best thing for her. Agreeing to stay another month, Bernardete promised to give them enough time to find a replacement for her. She hoped that they would not delay.

The days passed by, each one more difficult as the children tried to convince her to change her mind.

Finally, the date for her departure arrived. She said goodbye to the family who, in the past year had become her own - to begin a new chapter in her life. She could still hear the youngest children sobbing as she walked away and forced herself to not look back – she did not want them to see her crying too.

Those children remained in her heart and prayers forever.

A Destiny Unfolds...

Now in her new job, Bernardete was very content. As Isabel had said, she was immediately given a room within the staff hostel and soon got to know the other girls who also resided along her floor. They all shared a kitchen and a sitting room and so spent a lot of time together both in and away from their place of work.

She enjoyed the work – her colleagues were very friendly and each day was filled with laughter. She was surprised to realise how relaxed everything was – the doctors were very good-humoured and often stopped to share a joke with the staff who served them.

Bernardete found herself with more freedom and so immediately enrolled on an English course at the local college for foreign students. She had always been fascinated by other cultures and wanted to learn as many languages as possible - already having picked up basic French from the family she had worked for over the last year.

Most of her new colleagues and housemates were from other European countries including Spain, Poland, Italy and even her own, Portugal. They too were studying English at the same college and Bernardete was happy to be amongst girls with similar backgrounds to her own. All of them - though fiercely patriotic of their own homelands, recognised the importance of integration within the country that was now to be their home and were determined to fit in. That meant both learning to write - and to speak, fluent English.

In the evenings, they would sit together in the communal lounge to complete the homework they had been set. These sessions would often end up with the girls collapsing into uncontrollable fits of laughter – as they ended up mocking each other's interpretation of the words they were trying - unsuccessfully, to recite!

Bernardete was surprised to see that her wages were so much better than before and she was soon able to pay back the debt of her passage. She was also able to send more money back home to her mother – she was very glad about that. As a bonus, she had extra for herself and enjoyed more time off than before. Accepting this job had definitely been the right decision and she was very happy.

Now that she was working amongst those in the medical profession, Bernardete recalled her childhood desire to become a nurse. She had always been a sickly child, contacting pleurisy at the age of twelve and subsequently, spent six months away from her family in a hospice. The illness had left her so weak that she had been unable to walk for a while, and so each day, the nurses had wheeled her outside to take in the mountain air, hoping it would heal her.

She had never forgotten their kindness and had grown up, hoping that she could follow in their vocation and help others as they had helped her. Unfortunately, her parents had not had the money necessary for her to study nursing in Madeira and so, she had reluctantly accepted that this was not to be her destiny.

Now, she could not believe the options available to her. With the encouragement of her friends, Bernardete put her name forward to be a student at the nursing school. To her own amazement, she was accepted and invited to begin her training, the following year. At last, everything was going in her favour and with joy in her heart, she thanked God for so many blessings.

She never knew it at that time, but in just a few months her plans would be shattered.

A Boy...

One early morning, Bernardete, on her usual route to work, noticed a young man walking towards her. He was obviously staring in her direction and she, suddenly feeling shy, averted her eyes as he approached.

"Excuse me," - she turned as he spoke – "do you know the way to King's Cross Station?" Bernardete paused to tell him that he was actually very near and as she herself was going in that direction, she offered to show him the way.

As they walked together, he asked her name and introduced himself. In that short distance, she learned that he was called Tony, was Italian and he told her that he ran a nightclub in Kensington with his brother. She had no reason to disbelieve him, he seemed nice and so Bernardete agreed to meet him later that day for a coffee. She was quite flattered that he was interested in her… he was very well dressed and handsome, with thick dark hair and large brown eyes.

After work as arranged, they met and, sitting together in a local café, chatted about themselves, for some hours. Tony was keen to know about her background and family and so, finding herself at ease in his company, she agreed to go for a meal the following week. He was very attentive and seemed genuinely keen to get to know her. When he told Bernardete that he was busy with his own business and therefore, would only be able to see her once a week, she accepted his explanation without question. Naively she believed him, understanding that he must have a lot of responsibility in his job. Anyway, she was too was busy herself - most evenings taken up, either studying or working.

In the meantime, Bernardete had continued to write to her mother. Excited, she would rush to the communal mailbox in the hostel whenever post arrived, hoping that there would be a letter for her, with news from home. She had recently been overjoyed, to receive a large photograph of her entire family, sat together in their best clothes. She knew that not one of them owned a camera - and that meant that they would have had to pay for this picture to be taken, by a photographer in a studio. She was touched that they had gone to this trouble - just for her.

Adoringly she gazed upon her mother, grandmother, brothers and sisters – sitting solemnly alongside her little nephews and the young niece whom she had yet to meet. Bernardete treasured the photograph, proudly displaying it in her room and pointing out each of her relatives to all of her friends.

Her older sister had given birth to a little girl soon after Bernardete had left Madeira and she had sent her a picture of the child. It was placed on the little table next to her bed - her statue of the Virgin Mother, constantly watching over it. In return, she had put on her own best clothes and posed in one of the little photo-booths nearby. She wanted them to see for themselves how well she was doing – she knew that her mother would appreciate it.

Bernardete continued to write home, her letters always reminding them that there was plenty of work in England and that she missed them very much. She hoped and prayed that this might eventually persuade someone to join her.

Her heart jumped, when she read one day that her mother had managed to convince her youngest sister - aged just nineteen, to join her in London. With the help of a sponsor, a job and accommodation was quickly arranged and Bernardete was blissfully happy when she arrived just a few weeks later. Although they lived some distance apart, the two sisters were able to meet on their days off and spent much of their free time together.

Meanwhile, their brother-in-law had also written to say that he too, wanted to come to England. Bernardete loved him dearly. He had been like her own brother, helping her to secure a tenancy on her mother's house in Funchal - and paying the rent when she couldn't. It also meant that her beloved older sister and baby niece would soon follow and so she immediately wrote back, promising to find him a job and lodgings. She was overjoyed!

Things seemed to be going so well. She had good friends and a job which she loved, as well as her sister close by. In additional to all this good fortune, she was also looking forward to beginning her nursing training in just a few months. At last, Bernardete felt a sense of home.

In the meantime, she had continued to meet with Tony and was spending more of her free time with him – or at least, whenever *he* was available to meet her. They became close and she never doubted his words when he said that he loved her and they would marry one day. Bernardete put her trust in him but sadly, he was not the man she thought.

One morning, Bernardete awoke feeling very unwell. She rushed to the bathroom and was terribly sick. Wondering what could be wrong, she lay on her bed and telephoned Tony who, immediately concerned, insisted on rushing over to the hostel and taking her to the nearest surgery.

When they arrived, she was asked a few questions and to provide a sample for some tests. The doctor had initially suggested that she might have a kidney infection so she was not too worried. What he said next was a total shock. Bernardete was going to be a mother! She was pregnant!

Immediately, she turned to Tony and her heart sank as she saw his face…it had quickly changed from one of concern to absolute horror. Straight away she knew her fate – he would abandon her and the baby and she would be all alone. She was scared and silently begged our Lady of Fátima to help her – She was her only hope.

Tony stopped calling. For two months, Bernardete suffered terrible morning sickness, often struggling to go into work - and frightened that someone would soon notice her condition. She didn't know what to do. She tried phoning but by the time four months had passed, found out that he had moved house. He hadn't even told her. Desperate, she went to his nightclub, asking around whether anyone had seen him. She described him as Italian, saying that he was the owner of the club... they had laughed in her face and told her that, although he was the owner, he was *not* Italian and that no-one knew for sure where he was from... And Tony was just a nickname he used.

She was furious with him – but also with herself. How could she have believed his lies? There were also rumours that he had a wife and two young children. He had totally deceived her.

Bernardete ran out, embarrassed and devastated that he could have been so cruel. Desperate and with nowhere to turn, she knew that she could not contemplate telling her family – she felt so ashamed. News would travel quickly back home and her mother's heart would be shattered. Plus – what she had done was a sin. Her soul was condemned...

A Voice of Hope...

In a daze - her vision obscured by tears, Bernardete walked and walked for hours, before heading back in the direction of the hostel. Finding herself outside King's Cross Station, she stood there alone, not able to return and face her friends. Oblivious to the crowds of people rushing past her, she made her way to the bridge and sadly looked down at the track below. Her heart was breaking and her mind told her that there was no other way. Silently she prayed for forgiveness. And prepared to jump.

All of a sudden, a woman's soft voice spoke gently in her ear, "Bernardete..."

Startled, she turned around, expecting to see someone beside her - but there was no-one remotely near.

"Bernardete..." – her name again. A voice so gentle and calm, that she closed her eyes for a moment before she heard it say, "I am always with you and will help you – do not do this."

She was confused. She looked around again – the voice had come, it seemed, from within her!

Suddenly, an overwhelming warmth began to rise up as if deep within her soul and she felt instantly elevated. She was no longer afraid – she did not understand what had happened, but those thoughts disappeared and elated, she turned and ran out of the station. Her tears were now those of joy.

Bernardete had received a miracle.

"Oh thank you! Thank you my Blessed Mother! I promise dear Mother, that if my baby is a girl, she will be named after you – Fátima! I put us both in your Hands and promise to raise her to love you always."

Bernardete walked home, contemplating the grace that had been given to her. She knew she had been saved and immediately felt a great love for the child growing within her.

Asking for protection, she vowed in that moment, to entrust her life - and that of her baby's, completely to God's Will.

Bernardete carried on as before, now confident that she would be alright, whatever happened. She was, however, worried about peoples' reaction and so continued to hide her pregnancy for a while. But with each passing day, she was reminded of her situation - as her clothes grew tighter. Realising that she would not be able to disguise her condition for much longer, she knew that she would soon have to admit her pregnancy to her manager. Desperate for advice and finding herself alone one day with her closest colleague, Bernardete was suddenly overwhelmed, and breaking down - confided her secret.

Her friend, to Bernardete's surprise, did not react with shock and disgust but instead felt sorry for her and offered to help. She said that she knew of an agency which assisted girls in the same predicament and that they might be able to give her advice. Encouraged by her friend's promise to accompany her, Bernardete agreed to go and see them the next day.

When they arrived, the two girls were directed to a small private room where a smiling middle aged woman invited them warmly to sit down. She introduced herself and very gently, encouraged Bernardete to talk. Her name was Victoria and she told her that she had met many girls like her and that she should not feel ashamed. Attentively, she listened as Bernardete with a trembling voice, told her story.

Victoria reassured her that she would help. She proceeded to look through some files before pausing at one in particular. Turning to Bernardete, she said, "I might have a solution. I have a request here from a very well-off couple who are looking for someone just like you to work for them as a domestic maid. They are very busy people and often away on business - so they need someone who will look after their home and help out with housework." She went on, "The gentleman is the Chairman of a very important company and he travels a lot so, in all honesty, I think his wife is after a companion too. They have a very big house in North London and you would be expected to live in."

She looked up, "What do you think?"

Bernardete was doubtful. Why would these people want a pregnant girl in their home? She asked the woman the same. Victoria explained that they were charitable people who wanted to help girls like her. "From what I understand," she looked down at the file... "They are looking for someone reliable who is not going to just leave – and they realise that not many people will give an unmarried mother a job so leaving is unlikely… until you have the baby of course. Then, I suppose – you would return." She waited for Bernardete's reaction.

"Can I suggest we make an appointment for you to have an interview with them?" Victoria looked at her kindly. Bernardete felt that she could not refuse – what other options did she have? She was amazed to see that rather than judging her, Victoria had endeavoured to put forward a solution and so how could she refuse? As she got up to leave, Victoria assured her that she would receive a phone call confirming arrangements, as soon as she had spoken to the couple.

Heading back towards the hostel - and against the advice of her friend, Bernardete decided to try the club one more time, to look for Tony. It was early afternoon and so the main doors were still closed to the public. Bernardete knew that the side entrance would be open for deliveries and so she went in that way, quickly scanning the room for any sign of him.

There he was!

"Bernardete!" He exclaimed, surprised to see her there. "I'm sorry I haven't been to see you, I have been so busy…" She didn't let him continue – there was no way she was going to listen to his excuses. She was so angry!

"I don't believe you! I have been here so many times to look for you – you never phoned and you never answer my calls! Look how you left me!" She was hurt and sadly asked him why he didn't care for her anymore. Once again, Tony tried to tell her that he had been busy and of course he cared - but she could tell that he was humiliated to have been confronted in this way – and in his place of work. His colleagues were now watching them and embarrassed, he tried to lead Bernardete towards his office and away from their view.

She was tired. Reluctantly she asked him if he could at least help her with some money so that she could buy a few things in preparation for the baby.

"I will – I promise! I don't have any cash with me – and I have a meeting today so I can't go to the bank… but I promise, I will call you tomorrow!"

Bernardete left. How she wished she could believe him. That evening, Victoria telephoned to tell her that Lady Philips[1] was willing to meet her – it was settled.

---

[1] Name changed

A Helping Hand...

At 2pm the next day, Bernardete nervously waited for the bus which would take her to St. John's Wood.

Turning into the road on which the couple lived, she was immediately impressed at the beautiful tall white houses, each with expensive looking cars parked outside. Could she really live in a place like this herself?

She had now arrived at the address which Victoria had given her over the telephone. Anxiously, she stepped up to the door and rang the bell.

A tall, handsome woman greeted her with a beaming smile and saying "Hello Bernardete! So nice to see you!" she beckoned her inside. Feeling encouraged by the warm welcome, Bernardete stepped in and followed Lady Philips as she walked ahead and into a large, open kitchen.

"Do sit down," the lady pulled out a chair for her. "I shall just make us both a cup of coffee and then we can have a lovely chat and get to know each other."

Bernardete sat down as instructed and taking the coffee offered to her, smiled shyly – she didn't really know what to say.

Lady Philips sensed the young woman's lack of confidence and so she led the conversation, asking her lots of questions. She seemed a lovely person and was clearly keen to know all about Bernardete. She looked shocked - and even became quite teary-eyed, when she heard about Bernardete's poor upbringing and the loss of her father.

Impressed that this young woman in front of her had made the brave decision to travel all alone in order to help her family, Lady Philips decided straight away that she wanted to help her. They spoke for a long time, then she said, "Bernardete – you are a very brave young woman. I really like you and think we will get along wonderfully! I would love you to come and work for me. If you agree, you can start whenever you are able. We can look after each other can't we?"

Smiling, she told Bernardete that her husband was away for work, but that she would love them to meet. "Would you be able to come back next week?" she asked. "He will be back then."

It was settled. Bernardete had a new job.

A week passed and as agreed, she went back to the house, to meet Sir Philips. He – just like his wife, greeted her warmly and Bernardete felt immediately at ease in his company.

With his wife beside him, he chatted to the young woman as if they were old friends. Lady Philips had obviously already filled him in on her background and he commented that she had been incredibly brave. Together, they discussed her pregnancy and assured her that there would be a job and home for both her - and the baby, for as long as she wanted.

Bernardete left them that day feeling blessed. God had once again intervened and delivered a way forward and with it - hope of a secure future, for herself and her child.

That evening, Bernardete sat in her room – still hoping - but not expecting – Tony to call. He didn't.

It was now time to tell her manager about her decision and so, after her shift the next day, she knocked on her supervisor's door. Slowly explaining her situation, Bernardete told Maureen that she realised she would not be able to continue working at UCH - and was therefore handing in her notice. Maureen was sympathetic and begged her to reconsider.

"Please don't leave because of this! We all love you here – the doctors won't want you to go – they adore you! You could stay and we can help you to have the baby adopted. You will be free then and you could then continue with your dream to become a nurse! Please don't throw your life away!"

Bernardete was shocked. How could anyone consider giving up their own child? She began to cry and Maureen quickly rushed to her side. In between sobs, Bernardete responded, "Give my baby away? No – I can't! I will go to the end of the world – even starve – but my baby will be with me always!"

Maureen was immediately sorry for her suggestion and comforted her, apologising profusely. She promised to support Bernardete's decision and to provide her with an excellent reference.

Later that evening, Bernardete went to Tony's nightclub one more time. He wasn't there. Over the next few days, she rang him persistently but to no avail - until with a heavy heart, she accepted that he just wasn't interested.

She would have to do this alone. Her faith in the message she had received that sad day at the station, would give her strength.

It was the beginning of August, and Bernardete, was now nearly five months pregnant. Sad to be leaving, she eventually worked out her notice at the Hospital. She left behind all the friends she had made there - none of them knowing the real reason for her departure.

She had asked her best friend Isabel, to help her take her belongings over to St. John's Wood. Isabel by now knew that Bernardete was pregnant, and had been very supportive - even buying little gifts for the baby.

When they arrived at the house, Sir and Lady Philips were standing at the door and welcomed them both inside. "Come in dear! We are so glad you are finally here!" Isabel looked on in amazement as Lady Philips said, "Come with me! I'll take you straight up to your flat - and your friend can help you settle in whilst I make you some refreshments!"

Isabel was astonished! "A flat?" she exclaimed.

"Oh yes dear – we couldn't expect Bernardete to stay in one room with a small baby could we? She will have everything she needs – it will be so lovely to have a child here again!"

Lady Philips told them on the way upstairs, that she had only had one daughter and that she was now married and lived some distance away from her parents. The girls understood from her expression that she was quite lonely – the house was big and her husband was often away so she clearly spent a lot of time on her own.

Once at the top of the house, Bernardete and Isabel were shown into a small apartment. As she ushered them inside, Lady Philips watched the girls as they looked around, shocked at the space. The flat had its own living area, furnished and including a television set! A doorway led to a small bedroom and leading from that, a shower room. In the corner of the sitting room was a tiny kitchenette – it seemed that Bernardete would have everything she needed and more!

Bernardete was thrilled and rushed to embrace her new employer. Overjoyed, she said "God bless you! I can't believe it – you are so kind!" Laughing and hugging her in return, Lady Philips told her to unpack and left the two girls happily taking everything in.

Just a few hours later, Bernardete lay in a new bed – in new surroundings and thanked the Virgin Mary once again for coming to her aid. She prayed for her family and friends as usual – but this time, added two new names to her list. Sir and Lady Philips, who had opened their hearts - and their home to a lonely mother and her unborn child.

Bernardete easily settled into her role, often working alongside Lady Philips to complete a range of household chores. She was very happy and the two quickly became more than employer and maid – they became good friends too.

She was given every Sunday off and would sometimes use this time to visit her youngest sister, who had now started in a different job and was living much closer.

Occasionally, her brother-in-law would visit her at the house. When she knew that he was coming, Bernardete would often keep her own plate of food warm in the oven for him.

She thought it strange that, despite their obvious wealth, her employers were quite stingy with money and would only buy enough food for their requirements. Because of this, Bernardete never felt able to ask for an extra plate so that she could offer him a meal. Instead, she went without herself in order to make sure that he ate. She knew that he was saving every spare penny in order to return to Madeira and collect his wife and daughter to bring them back with him to England – and was afraid that he would not be eating properly.

Bernardete never knew it then, but he had always been aware of her sacrifice for his sake and it would remain in his memory forever. He would, unbeknown to him at the time, come to repay her for this selfless act of kindness many years later - in the only way he could.

One Sunday evening, Bernardete was waiting at the bus stop when a car pulled up and stopped right in front of her. Feeling vulnerable on her own, Bernardete tried to ignore the young man, as he leant across the passenger seat to speak to her. "Hey! I know you! Come – do you want a lift?" Peering cautiously into the car, she thought she recognised him from somewhere but wasn't sure...

Her pregnancy was obvious by now and crossly, she told him to go away – could he not see? "But I know you!
74

I've seen you at your sister's! Come on – you shouldn't be standing in the cold like that – let me drop you home. It's ok!"

Realising then that - of course, *that's* how she knew his face, Bernardete apologised. It was freezing - and her legs and back were aching, so she gratefully accepted his offer.

The young man drove her home, chatting casually about his work and asking about hers. She was cautious when he asked if she had a boyfriend, immediately embarrassed to admit that, no, she was single and pregnant. But he didn't react – instead saying that he would like to take her out on her next day off. Shocked, Bernardete stared at him. "Don't you see how I am? Why would you want to take me out?" Undeterred, he told her that he had noticed her before - and it didn't matter to him.

Considering what she had already been through, Bernardete was suspicious. There was no way that any man would want her – and carrying somebody else's baby too? It was impossible.

Before too long, they arrived at Norfolk Road and - as he opened the passenger door, he asked her to think about seeing him again. Never really expecting him to call, Bernardete gave in and writing it down quickly, handed him her telephone number.

She was incredibly surprised when he did ring – and continued to do so, always with genuine concern for both her and her baby.

His name was Paul.

A Mother & Baby Home...

By now, Bernardete was seven months into her pregnancy. It was becoming more difficult for her to work and Lady Philips could see that even the smallest tasks were leaving the young woman exhausted. Taking pity, she would insist that Bernardete rest. Instead, she herself would bring up cups of tea and carried out much of the housework herself. Whenever she felt unwell, Bernardete's worried employer would take her own car, and drive her to the doctor's surgery.

She was a wonderful compassionate woman and Bernardete would never forget her kindness.

Together, they had discussed what would happen, as Bernardete's time grew closer. Having researched the options, they had realised that there were in fact - not many at all. When Lady Philips suggested the young woman go into an institution for the six weeks leading up to the expected delivery date, Bernardete agreed – how could she expect them to look after her when she was barely able to do her job? They promised that she would return to them straight afterwards and so, it was decided that she should move into a mother and baby home.

These homes were places specifically for unmarried, expectant women who had nowhere else to go. Generally paid for by the state, they were usually run by religious institutions - such as the Roman Catholic Church.

Bernardete felt nervous as she had no idea what these homes were like, however she understood that it was for the best under the circumstances.

The day came far too quickly and as they put her into a taxi outside their home, Sir and Lady Philips gave her a hug. Promising that everything would be alright, they assured her that, both her job - and the flat would be waiting for her when she returned. Tears began to fill her eyes as Bernardete turned sadly to wave goodbye.

It was a freezing cold morning on 22 October 1966 when Bernardete arrived at the Convent of the Sacred Heart at 34 Highgate West Hill in North London. Pushing her way through a large iron gate, she looked around. The grounds were vast – several buildings surrounded a large stone statue of the Sacred Heart of Jesus which stood with His arms outstretched, in the centre.

Part of the convent was allocated to the Mother and Baby Home. This was called St. Pelagia's and it was run by the Catholic Sisters of the Sacred Heart of Jesus and Mary. Across from this in a separate building, stood St. Joseph's maternity home. The first was where expectant mothers would stay until they were ready to give birth and the second, where they would actually have their babies and then remain for the following six weeks.

Bernardete followed a sign indicating the direction of the admissions office and finding herself outside, nervously knocked on the door. She jumped as it was opened immediately by a stern faced nun - who ushered her quickly inside.

Bernardete was asked to confirm her name and then, without a word - the nun turned and walked away. With no indication of whether she should follow, Bernardete stood on the spot until she was harshly told, "What are you waiting for? Hurry up! The Mother does not have all day!"

The nun was impatiently standing outside one of the rooms leading off from the large hallway. The door was shut with a prominent sign on the front which read *Do Not Enter*. Obediently, she quickly rushed to the nun's side and shaking, waited as she knocked sharply on the door.

"Enter."

Bernardete walked in behind the other woman. Directly in front of them was a large mahogany desk - almost obscured by messy piles of folders and other papers. Seated behind it was a nun, dressed from head to toe in a full habit, only the roundness of her face visible. Without a hint of welcome, she told Bernardete to sit. Then, with a brush of her hand in the air, she casually dismissed her colleague, still standing beside the door.

"I am the Mother Superior. *You* shall call me Mother". She peered down her spectacles at the nervous woman opposite her. Rudely shuffling the documents in front of her, she ignored Bernardete as she proceeded to search for the relevant paperwork.

Taking that moment to glance around the room, Bernardete noticed dozens of holy pictures adorning each wall. Directly above the nun's desk hung a large, imposing crucifix – the figure of Jesus twisted in pain. His eyes seemed to know her own suffering as they looked sadly into hers...

"So *Bernardete*... why are you here?" The way she said the girl's name sounded almost sarcastic. Bernardete looked at her, confused by the question.

"I am here to have my baby..."

"NO!"

Bernardete jumped as the woman stood up, both palms flat on the desk as she shouted, "YOU are here because you are a sinner! YOU have sinned against God and brought shame upon your church and your family! WE will do all that is necessary to provide you with opportunities - to atone for that sin – but ultimately, it is not in our hands to grant your soul mercy. *That* is up to God." With a heavy thud, as if exhausted from her own outburst, the nun sat back down.

Bernardete began to tremble as tears started to sting her eyes. She felt so ashamed.

Speaking in a harsh voice, the Mother Superior impatiently snapped, "It's too late for that *now*, isn't it?" Once again, she ignored the girl's obvious distress and picked up a sheet of paper, pushing it roughly towards her.

"Right. Sign this. It gives *us* – the Sisters of the Sacred Heart – full responsibility for your welfare and that of your child, leading up to the birth and immediately afterwards. In return, you will be expected to abide by our rules, respect our routine and work - to the highest standard, in payment for our generosity." She stopped to take in Bernardete's reaction... "Were it not for the church and the Holy Sisters here, where would sinners such as yourself, be?"

Bernardete stared at her. She could not believe that someone supposed to represent Christ, could be so maliciously unkind and - for just a moment, wondered if it was conceivable for her to just get up and walk straight out of there...

Instead, she reached out, picked up the pen and signed.

For the next few minutes, Bernardete sat there, barely listening as the woman recited the rules of the Home.

"All 'inmates' – and that includes *you* – are assigned duties on a rota system. You must commence these directly after breakfast every day. You will finish once those tasks are

82

complete to our satisfaction. Remember, this is not a hotel and you will work for your keep – any excuses or laziness will not be tolerated."

She went on to say, "Forming relationships with each other is discouraged. Remember the reason you are here. It is *not* to make friends – and I can assure you that you are unlikely to speak again once you have left. You may have visitors on your day off but..." she paused, looking directly at Bernardete. "I doubt that you have anyone who will *want* to visit, given the circumstances."

Bernardete's fear of the woman was now turning to anger. What did she know? She knew nothing of the kind couple who employed her... or her sister who would certainly come and see her. Or Paul...

Rising suddenly from her chair, the Mother Superior called out in a loud voice and the nun who had shown Bernardete into the room, immediately appeared.

"Show her to the dormitory," she said. "Oh – and *Bernardete!*" Once again, she emphasised her name using the same spiteful tone. "You will *not* use your own name here. You may choose another, but do not disclose yours to any of the other inmates. You may go."

With that, she waved her hand to dismiss both women and turned her back. Bernardete, led by the nun, stepped out into the hallway and - with her head low and tears falling freely, followed her up the large staircase to the floor above. The dormitory was large with several beds laid out in a row, each neatly made and identical to the one next to it. There were no personal artefacts on show to identify any individual – it all seemed to Bernardete, very cold and clinical.

As she looked around the room, she noticed a young girl who was kneeling with her back to them and vigorously scrubbing the wooden floor. Holding her lower back, the girl slowly turned around and Bernardete saw that her belly was huge. Surely, she shouldn't be working so hard at that late stage? She looked ready to drop! Bernardete looked at the nun beside her expecting some acknowledgement of the girl's discomfort - but there was none. The nun acted as if she hadn't noticed at all. With a timid smile in the direction of her new roommate, the girl turned back to get on with her task.

Bernardete was quickly allocated a bed. With barely enough time to push her case underneath it, the nun rushed her back out of the room. Impatiently, she said "Now you must begin your work. There is no slacking here – and enough time left today for you to accustom yourself with what is expected – before we eat later on. I assume that you ate before you came?" She did not wait for Bernardete to respond as she led her straight back down the stairs - and into a large kitchen.

Handing her an apron to put on, Bernardete was instructed to begin by washing a pile of enormous pots – clearly recently used to cook the lunchtime meal. She felt sick when she looked inside, her stomach heaving and the sight of the remnants of food she would now have to scrape. If she had felt hungry, she certainly didn't now.

The nun noticed her displeasure and said, "Do not think you can slack here! Remember – hard labour is part of the penance you must do for the sin you have committed."

The days passed, each one worse than the day before. The work forced on the young women was exhausting and began even before they had eaten breakfast which was served at 7am. If any of them arrived just a few minutes late, they received such a glaring reception from the nuns that their appetites soon disappeared!

In small groups, the young women on that particular part of the rota would take turns to lay the tables, serve the food or wash up. Each plate, pot and utensil had to then be put away in its own allocated place. Some of the heavier pots were on high shelves – no easy task for the heavily pregnant girls and the nuns watched as they struggled – scolding them whenever they groaned in discomfort.

Straight from breakfast, they would go on to begin the individual chores assigned to each of them. Heaving heavy loads of laundry, they would wash, bleach, dry and iron – many of the items were badly stained and included nappies from the babies in St. Joseph's. These would have to be scrubbed by hand and disinfected until they were spotless. Other girls would collect scrubbing brushes and mops, before getting down on their knees to clean each corridor and step.

At night, some of the girls would have to make up bottles for the babies in order to help those who had recently given birth – there was no let-up in the work they had to do.

Bernardete suffered constant aches in her legs and one day, nearly collapsed with exhaustion. A doctor was summoned and soon discovered, that she was severely deficient in iron. The frightened girl was dismayed to be told that she would require a weekly injection until long after her delivery – she was terrified of needles and hated it when the time came again for each one.

With her eyes closed tight, she would recite several Hail Marys inside her head in an attempt to disassociate herself from the discomfort and fear that she felt.

On Sundays, some of the women would accompany the sisters to mass at the nearby church of St. Joseph's. Many eyes would be upon them as they walked in – the other parishioners looking disapprovingly at their large tummies. It was obvious to them that the girls were from the Mother and Baby Home and they made no attempt to hide their disgust.

The nuns would warn them to sit at the back of the church so as not to distract the *righteous* - reminding them also, that they were not permitted to receive communion. Bernardete believed that the shame and embarrassment she was made to feel was justified and sadly accepted this as part of her penance.

Many of the other girls went to mass the first week… and never again.

All of these vulnerable young women were treated with disdain and the nuns showed no sympathy to complaints of pain or tiredness. Although it was permitted, they were discouraged from leaving the walls of the convent.

Constantly reminded, the girls understood that people would look at them - and know their sin and their shame.

At first, Bernardete defied the nuns and would go into Highgate village to escape the confines of the Home for a few hours. However, as the weeks passed and the baby grew inside her, she became more aware of the disapproving whispers and, ashamed, begun to stay indoors. The women she came across would deliberately look at her hand to see if she was wearing a wedding ring and she knew what they were thinking when they realised that she wasn't. They made her feel like a criminal.

Bernardete wept most nights, praying that the baby would be born soon so that she could leave this awful place.

Despite the rules and within the limitations of their time, the girls became friendly with one another – after all, they each shared the same fears about giving birth and the future.

Bernardete discovered that most of the girls at the home were Irish, sent here by their families who - ashamed, wanted to hide them away. She could see the sadness in these girls' eyes as they quietly accepted the abusive insults of the nuns and felt very sad that even their own families had abandoned them. They were called sinners and dirty and told constantly that they had brought shame upon their families and persistently reminded that, if it wasn't for the Catholic Church, they would be on the streets. Meekly accepting this – the girls knew that it was probably true.

Many of the nuns were so obviously cruel that Bernardete had to remind herself that this was nothing to do with her faith. She knew that her God was a loving and forgiving father. One day, He too would judge these very people who were poised and ready to throw stones at these sad, helpless girls who had turned to them for compassion. They chose to ignore Jesus' example of love and forgiveness and instead, they condemned these sad helpless girls to more misery.

The young women were discouraged from socialising but, alone in their bedroom or in the sitting room after their chores were finished, they would quietly confide their fears with one another. Sometimes, they were even able to laugh at the actions of some of the fiercer nuns and would imitate their expressions – collapsing in fits of giggles before being told to angrily to 'shush' by whoever was supervising them at the time.

Bernardete realised that many of the girls had been forced to change their names at the request of their very own families. This was in order to keep their pregnancies a secret. But although the Mother Superior had told her to do the same, she was defiant, and refused to answer to anything else. Her own mother had chosen her name and she would not be called by another. Ignoring them when they spoke to her, the nuns had looked at her in disgust – how could she think that she was entitled to carry the name of a saint with such a sin on her soul?

Some of the girls were forced to return to their homes afterwards and to carry on as before - as if nothing had happened. Bernardete had watched them, their hearts clearly broken, as they were made to take their own babies to the Catholic Children's Society in Ladbroke Grove. There, eager new parents were waiting to adopt these little children – so happy were they that they never gave a thought to the birth mother's agony in handing them over. Within days, these poor young women had disappeared from St Pelagia's – all memory of them extinguished. They were almost immediately replaced by new girls, pregnant and with eyes wide and frightened as they entered the home – just the same as those before them.

During her time there, Bernardete had once peeked into the nursery and gazed at these sweet little babies, all in rows. Each of them loved by a mother who would soon have to give them up. Both society and the nuns had them convinced that they did not deserve to keep their children – and were selfish if they tried to deny it the chance of a better life - with two loving parents. Saddened at this thought, Bernardete again thanked God that she had a place to go and a job to support her own baby, once it was born.

Bernardete began her contractions on 12th December 1966 – her own 28th birthday, and these pains continued for almost a week before the nuns begrudgingly allowed her to stop work.

She was down on her knees, waxing the parquet floor of the entrance hall when, on 18th December, her waters finally broke. Distressed and with sweat pouring down her face from the pain, she was taken across the courtyard and over to the maternity unit to prepare for the birth - the nun accompanying her, clearly annoyed that the floor would need doing again.

Her labour was agony, with no pain relief or comforting hand to hold. Terrified at what was happening to her body, Bernardete could only pray for it to end.

At 5am on Monday 19th December 1966, Bernardete's baby girl was born.

That baby was me.

The next day, Lady Philips was informed by the Mother Superior, that Bernardete had had the baby and she immediately rushed over to see her. She looked on, as the new mother gazed down proudly at her little girl.

"Oh, Bernardete! She is beautiful! Look at all that lovely hair! And what amazing eyes – she's already so alert! What are you calling her?"

Bernardete replied, "Her name is Fátima. I named her after our Lady of Portugal, who helped me so much when I was in need."

Lady Philips held the child, stroking her little head - which was covered in lovely black hair. Her big brown eyes stared up at the stranger, but she didn't cry at all.

"So, when will you be permitted to leave? We can't wait to have you back with this little one!"

Bernardete promised to let her know once she had spoken to the Sister-in-charge.

She really hoped it would be soon.

Within a day of delivery, she was back doing her chores. The nuns, at least had the grace to lighten her duties, but for someone who had just given birth and therefore still in great discomfort, it was cruel not to excuse them at least, for a few days. There was no time allowed for recovery or rest – the only exception was where something had gone wrong in delivery - and the mother had been sent to the nearby hospital.

Bernardete was forced to put her baby in the nursery with the others and informed that, she must only go to her at when she needed to be fed and changed. With barely enough time allocated to do this, the mothers were hurried back to their chores - sometimes with the sounds of their babies still crying because they hadn't taken enough milk - or been winded properly.

The new mothers were instructed not to breast feed as it would take too long and interfere with their work. None of these young women realised how painful it would be to deny what was natural and in those early days, suffered greatly. Their bodies would react to their baby's distant cries from the nursery and so they were given tablets to dry out their milk. Many would live to suffer the consequences of this and in fact, Bernardete herself – many years later, suffered a cyst caused by a blocked milk duct. She ended up hospitalised because at that time all those years before, she had not been permitted to breast feed and her treatment then had been so poor. This rule was intended, to prevent the natural bond between mother and baby. The nuns would have argued that it was for their own good as it would make separation less traumatic when the time came to give up their babies. In reality and in most cases, the bond was probably there from the moment their children was conceived.

Each mother quickly came to recognise her own baby's cries and - distressed, they would beg to be allowed to go to them. The nuns would scold them and refuse. They did not permit them to comfort the little ones and told them instead that they were being selfish and to leave the parenting to those who would eventually take them.

Bernardete felt sad for these girls – she knew that most of them did not want to give their babies up for adoption. The fact that this did not apply to her, did nothing to change the attitude of the nuns - she too was forbidden to visit her baby outside feeding times.

The new mothers would help one another by secretly checking on each other's babies whenever it was their own turn to go to the nursery.

It was a cruel and unforgiving existence. Bernardete realised she had to get her child away from there – and soon. As soon as she felt able, she approached one of the sisters to ask when she could leave. The nun crossly snapped at her, "When someone agrees to adopt your baby! *Then* you can get back to your life!"

Bernardete was shocked and grabbed her arm! "What do you mean? No-one is going to adopt her – I am not giving her away! She is mine and mine alone!"

The nun stepped back in surprise. With a face like thunder, she immediately turned around and Bernardete - now terrified, watched her as she marched quickly towards the Mother Superior's office.

Frantic, she felt in her pockets for a coin and rushed over to the payphone in the hallway. She was shaking as she dialled Lady Philips' number and barely able to control her fingers. Thankfully, her call was answered straight away and Bernardete, in between sobs, told her boss what the nuns were expecting her to do.

"They want me to give up my baby!" she cried, her voice hysterical.

Promising to speak to the Mother Superior directly, Lady Philips assured Bernardete that she must not worry – they would - as promised, help her look after the child.

"It will all be alright – I will make sure that you shall both be back here as soon as it can be arranged."

Bernardete felt relieved – she knew that Lady Philips could be trusted to keep her word and so she went straight to the nursery, even though she knew that it was against the rules. She picked up her little girl and held her close – she didn't care if they caught her. There was no way they were having her child.

Within just a few minutes the nun reappeared, this time accompanied by the Mother Superior herself. They confirmed that she and the baby would be able to leave in a few days – Bernardete was so relieved!

"And would you like to baptise the child before you both leave us? It is our moral duty to ensure that she has this sacrament before we discharge her permanently to your care..." The senior nun looked expectantly at Bernardete.

She didn't dare refuse. Of course she wanted her baby christened – and soon, but she was confused at how quickly their attitude had changed! She suspected that Lady Philips had promised to make a donation if they agreed to push the necessary paperwork through quickly – she had heard from the other women that 'money talked' in this establishment.

Bernardete didn't care – she was overjoyed. She was going to be leaving soon and most importantly, with her precious baby. Once again, her Mother in Heaven had intervened and saved her.

She smiled at the nun in front of her and said yes, she would be very grateful. She certainly did not want to antagonise them at this point and was pleased that they had offered to arrange it for her. She believed that a child should be baptised as soon as possible after birth.

Arrangements were made in haste so that the christening could take place during Midnight Mass on Christmas Eve, in the Convent's Church of St Joseph.

Christmas was close - even the sisters were more cheerful as they decorated the home with garlands and a tree. Bernardete felt excited for the double celebration as she also knew that she would be leaving very soon afterwards.

Only one thing made her sad. She did not have a new white christening robe for the baptism. Instead, she dressed her baby in a pretty little pink crocheted cardigan which she had brought with her into the home.

Sleeping peacefully, the tiny little girl at just six days old, resembled an angel. Her mother felt so blessed that her baptism would take place on this special night and carried her proudly into the church.

Standing beside Bernardete, was her brother-in-law. Although her sister was still in Madeira, she was due to join her husband in the New Year and so, she had asked them both to be Godparents to her baby.

In his wife's absence - and with nothing else to offer, her Godfather removed his own gold bracelet and gently wrapped it twice around the wrist of the child.

The bond between the little girl and her godparents would last a lifetime.

A Proposition & a Proposal...

On 28th December, on a freezing cold day with the ground saturated with snow, Bernardete carried her nine day old daughter and finally left St Pelagia's Home to return to the house in St. John's Wood. Their life together could now begin.

Sir and Lady Philips were clearly very happy to have a small baby in their home and showered her with attention. Bernardete returned to her duties the next day, beginning at 6am with the baby's feed and then down to the kitchen to prepare breakfast for the couple. Whilst they ate, she would quickly run upstairs to see if the child was alright. She was a good baby who hardly cried. Bernardete would then return to the housework - leaving the television on quietly to keep the baby company. Fátima would look at it, mesmerised by the moving images as she lay on her mother's bed. Whenever she came back to check, Bernardete would find her contentedly gurgling to herself.

If Bernardete ever heard her crying, she would rush back to her room - often surprised to find Lady Philips already there with the baby in her arms and comforting her. She felt so happy that the couple really cared for the child and was very grateful for their kindness and support. The days passed quickly and both mother and baby settled into a happy routine.

Bernardete was even happier when at last, her eldest sister arrived from Madeira, early on in the New Year. Now living nearby with her husband and own little daughter, she was besotted with her new niece and they often spent weekends together.

Sometimes, Bernardete would meet Paul and they would take the baby to the park. He quickly became very attached to the little girl and she in turn, soon recognised him - smiling whenever she saw his face.

Six months went by and, one day, Lady Philips asked Bernardete if she could speak to her about something important. Immediately nervous, she wondered if they were going to dismiss her. What would she do? She had nowhere else to live and - without any money, how would she be able to look after her baby? Bernardete could do nothing but turn again to our Lady of Fátima in prayer. She prayed all night – she knew that Sir Philips was returning in the morning and she would be summoned then.

As expected, the next day Bernardete was called into his office where his wife was already waiting. They invited her to sit down, telling her that they had a proposition for her. Bernardete didn't even know what that meant, but their serious manner made her feel very afraid. Nervously, she did as they asked.

"Bernardete, we realise that things have been very difficult for you and hope that we have helped you - as you have helped us. We know that your life could have been different, had you not had a child. We are sorry that you have not been able to fulfil your ambitions as you had hoped when you first arrived in England. Of course, we admire you for your courage and determination – but feel that life has not been fair on you… "

Bernardete said nothing. She stared at them, tears ready to fall as she wondered where this was going…

Sir Philips walked around the desk and placed his hand gently upon her shoulder.

"We should like to adopt your baby! You, of course, are welcome to stay and work for us if that is your wish – you could see her every day - but we would take full responsibility for her and your life could go on! You could do whatever you wanted to do when you first came – perhaps follow your dream of becoming a nurse!"

Smiling at her, he continued, "you know how much we already love her and we can promise you that she would want for nothing!"

By now, Bernardete couldn't stop the tears and they flowed freely down her cheeks as she looked at him in shock. Lady Philips, surprised at this reaction, rushed quickly to her side. "Oh Bernardete – please don't cry! Think about it – please! She would have everything she ever needed and a secure home always – please consider it!"

Bernardete was dismayed. Had this been their plan from the very beginning? She could not imagine that this had been the reason for their kindness – they had always been so supportive and had always known how desperate she had been to keep her child. Why would they suggest such a thing?

"I don't want to think about it – please don't ask this of me! You know I can't ever give my baby away – she is *everything* I have – she is my life! If you want me to leave, I will – but with my daughter! She will be poor but at least she will have her real mum to love her!"

The couple looked at her and instantly realised their error. Bernardete, now on her feet, continued. "Don't you see? It was bad enough for her father to abandon her! I will *never* do that – don't you see what she is to me?"

Sir Philips immediately apologised, ashamed that they had not considered her feelings – he had assumed that she would be grateful for a chance to get back her life. He assured her that - of course, they wanted her to stay and promised not to mention it again. Lady Philips hugged her and wiping her tears, told her to forget the conversation had ever taken place. Bernardete was apprehensive – she hoped that they had done this with a genuine desire to make her life easier and not for their own gain.

Convincing herself that they had just made a terrible mistake and did not intentionally wish to hurt her, Bernardete agreed to stay. They had got it all wrong and it was just a misunderstanding.

In time, Bernardete forgot the couple's proposition and things went back to how they were before. Balancing her work with bringing up her baby, she was happy. The couple now allowed her every weekend off, realising that she and the baby should spend more time amongst family and friends.

In the warmer evenings, Lady Philips and Bernardete would sit in the garden and fondly watch the little girl who was now attempting to crawl. She and her husband kept their promise and never again spoke about adoption - but continued to take great pleasure in Fátima's progress. They clearly loved her.

In the meantime, Bernardete had been seeing more of Paul. Although she had been initially afraid to get into another relationship after the way she was treated before, it was clear to her that, he was very different. He had never judged her - and was always by her side whenever she needed anything. More than that, he clearly cherished Fátima and did more for her than any father could – spoiling her with so much love and attention. For a man to take on someone else's child in that way, Bernardete knew that he was very special.

She decided to tell Lady Philips about him. Pleased to hear that she had found someone so wonderful, her boss told

Bernardete to invite Paul to the house - so that she could meet him. It was clear that she wanted to judge for herself if he was as decent a man as he had been described and - being very protective of the young woman, she would do anything to avoid seeing her hurt.

She was impressed when, the very next day, Paul arrived to meet her. Inviting him into her home, Lady Philips led him to the living room and together, the three sat down and chatted for several hours.

Lady Philips could tell that Paul's intentions were honest – he was a hard worker with his own business and – more importantly, was obviously devoted to Bernardete and the child. She could see immediately that the couple were happy and so, without any hesitation, promised that he could visit them whenever he wanted.

Although she had not needed her boss' approval, Bernardete felt pleased that Paul had made a great impression on someone she respected so much.

For a couple of months, everything was good. Except that Bernardete noticed Sir Philips spending more time at home – she wondered what was happening with his business but felt it wasn't her place to ask. Eventually it became clear as Lady Philips, once again asked to speak to her.

The woman sadly told Bernardete that they had decided to sell the house in London and relocate to Norfolk - where they had another property. Lady Philips suggested hopefully, that she might consider going with them – after all, they would still need help in the other house.

Bernardete was saddened by this news - could she really contemplate being separated once again from her family and Paul - especially after she finally felt part of something? She replied that she would need to tell her boyfriend and see whether he had an alternative… if not, she would go with them.

Of course, when she told Paul of their plan, he was adamant that she should not go. He said that they should get married, suggesting that they move in together until they had saved enough for a wedding. Overjoyed and now convinced of his commitment to her, Bernardete agreed.

She gently conveyed the news to her employer who reluctantly, accepted her decision. Bernardete was relieved. Although very sad to have to submit her notice to the couple who had helped her so much, she knew deep down that she would never again, be able to leave those she loved.

A Love that Saves...

Lady Philips was quite emotional, her feelings torn between sadness at losing Bernardete and the baby whom she had grown so fond of and joy - that they had found someone who truly loved them and would take care of them both.

Within just a month, she and her husband had left London and the young couple found a small flat to move into together.

Now with rent and bills to pay, Bernardete had to find another job to help Paul with the cost of living. She soon located a local nursery for the baby and began working as a chambermaid in a hotel in Notting Hill Gate.

The couple yearned for their own place and worked hard in order to build a future for themselves and their little girl.

Unfortunately, the new job meant that once again, she had to work weekends. Paul would look after the baby - who by now was walking. He would often take her to Hyde Park or Kensington Gardens to feed the ducks - whilst they waited for her mother to finish work. Strangers passing by them, often paused to admire the doting father with his happy, laughing little girl.

In order to make up the time he had sacrificed to look after the child, Paul would have to return to work after he had taken them safely home. He never complained and would often work until past 10pm – rescuing broken down vehicles in freezing weather or laying on the cold ground underneath a car in his garage.

He just wanted to do the best he could for his little family.

At the age of four, Fátima was enrolled into primary school at Normand Park in Fulham, not too far from Paul's garage. A nanny collected her from school until Bernardete's return from her job in West London.

By now, Bernardete's younger brother and sister had joined the other siblings in London and, even though she was destined to be an only child, Fátima never felt lonely. Surrounded by a close-knit extended family who all lived in the same street, there was always someone to look after the others' children.

She had many cousins - and at least one aunt or another would sit on the steps outside their home, watching over the youngsters as they played outside. Often it would be her Godmother who - busy with her latest embroidery, would look up to keep an eye on her young daughter, nephews and niece as they ran joyfully past without a care in the world. It was an idyllic childhood which Fátima and her cousins would remember fondly for years to come.

They were such happy days and Bernardete felt so blessed.

She often contemplated how lonely she had been and all the suffering she had endured in those earlier years... she had never imagined that she would get through them. But with her faith and a promise from our Lady of Fátima – she had endured and survived.

Yet there was one thing that still brought Bernardete sorrow. Her heart longed for her own mother whom she had walked away from so sadly, all those years before.

She had been devastated to hear that her beloved grandmother had died and added to the grief she felt was such sadness in the realisation that the last time she had seen her had been exactly that – the last time.

When Fátima was nearly five years old, Bernardete's greatest desire was realised. With air travel from Madeira now possible, Maria had decided to visit England, to see her beloved children whom she missed so much. The youngest brother, just eighteen, travelled with her and together, they arrived into the loving arms of their family.

Cuddling her youngest grand-daughter, Maria was pleased that her Bernardete had found love with such a good man. When she had discovered her daughter's situation as a single mother, it had made her so desperately sad to think of her, all by herself.

But God was good and had heard her prayers, in time bringing peace and stability to her life.

As she watched Paul lovingly carry the sleeping child to his car one late evening, her eyes filled with tears of gratitude and joy.

A month soon passed and the family bid an emotional goodbye to each other at Heathrow Airport. Maria had listened to her children's pleas to stay, but she was not yet ready to make such a huge transition. It would take a lot to adjust to the weather and the language - and she also had to think about her teenage son and her home in Madeira. Reluctantly, the family accepted that it was not to be – not yet, anyway.

By now, Bernardete and Paul had moved to a larger flat in Elephant & Castle. She was now working alongside two of her sisters as well as another friend who was also from Madeira. The women were lucky in that they were permitted to bring their children to work during the school holidays, which they often did. Their boss was very accommodating and preferred this option to having his staff take time off. Besides, there was plenty of room for them to sit quietly at the hotel – provided they were well-behaved.

Fully aware of this unusual privilege, the women constantly reminded their children to behave whilst on the premises – they knew that without it, they would have problems finding childcare and that would mean that they would probably have to stop working altogether. None of them could afford to do this. Although Paul would sometimes take Fátima along to the garage with him, Bernardete did not feel it an appropriate environment for a small girl – and she could not be expected to sit there in the cold all day long whilst her daddy worked.

Bernardete was grateful that her boss was so accommodating and so Fátima, often still sleepy and complaining at having to get up so early - would have to accompany her mother to work. Her grumpiness soon disappeared once she discovered that the other women had also brought their own children along and the girls spent many happy hours together exploring the hotel. Running from floor to floor, they would cheerfully interact with the regular guests - as well as the hotel owner. By now, they were all accustomed to the two little cousins and their friends.

Whether just eating toast and jam in the restaurant whilst drawing pictures – or sitting in the communal lounge watching the massive cinema sized television, the children entertained themselves quite easily - whilst their mothers got on with their jobs.

Sometimes, Fátima would persuade Bernardete to return to her Godmother's house, after they had finished work. Together, the four of them would catch the number 27 bus to Paddington - where she lived, stopping off first, to buy fresh bread and a cake for each of the girls on the way.

Paul never complained when Bernardete telephoned him – asking that he detour and pick them up after a hard day's work. His reward, a plate of steaming hot food cooked by his sister-in-law as soon as he arrived!

Whilst life was good, there was one problem. The couple were unhappy in their new home. Their flat was located on the second floor of a crowded housing estate, directly above East Street Market. Many of their neighbours were unfriendly and would not even attempt to hide their resentment at the 'foreigners' living in their block.

On many occasions, Paul would return home to find their fuses – which were located in the communal corridors, maliciously cut, and they would have no electricity until he had fixed them.

They also felt unable to allow their small daughter to play outside. The corridors were dirty with people arguing and sitting around in the stairwells - and they did not feel it was safe. On top of all this, the bustling market began at 5am with traders shouting and Lorries revving their engines, waking them up before the day had truly begun.

It was at that point that they decided to move and this time, they would try to buy a house of their own.

To complete their commitment to each other, the couple got married in a quiet little ceremony, with just Bernardete's older sister and brother-in-law as witnesses. Their daughters had been at school that day, and - oblivious to the reason for celebration, were excited as they accompanied their parents to a restaurant later that evening.

Bernardete would later remind Fátima about that meal when - accustomed to helping her mother out at home, the young child had instinctively started to clear the plates as soon as they had finished eating - ready to wash up! The adults watching her, had laughed so much!

With relief, the day finally came for them to leave and they headed off to their new home, situated in a small suburb of Ealing, West London. Over the years the couple had worked hard, saving every spare penny and so were luckily able to afford the little terraced property with its own small back garden.

As she stepped into the hallway, Bernardete blessed herself - she could never have foreseen such a wonderful day!

There had been times early on, when she had thought about Tony - wondering if her child ever crossed his mind. In those early months, he would have been able to locate her - if he had wanted to… but he had not ever tried, not even to offer financial support.

Bernardete felt sad to think that even if he had never loved *her*, he had never even been curious about Fátima.

She shook her head to dispel these thoughts from her mind. She was happy – and so was her daughter.

Soon the van arrived with their belongings, and together, the family unloaded the boxes, placing them into their relevant locations. Fátima was excited to have such a large bedroom and within minutes had disappeared to arrange her dolls and toys in their new home.

Bernardete was looking for a specific box. She had labelled it so that she could recognise it easily – she was keen to make sure that the items inside had arrived safely and in one piece.

The furniture was being stacked in the hallway and so, with nowhere yet to sit, Bernardete knelt on the floor to inspect the box in front of her.

Carefully, she lifted out her most treasured possessions. Her beloved blue crucifix and the triptych containing the little statue of our Lady of Fátima were unharmed.

Bernardete smiled with relief. Though they held no monetary value, these precious items had been her link to all she loved and a much needed comfort as she took that lonely journey, all those years before.

With every move to a different home, Bernardete had made sure that they took pride of place – the crucifix in her own room - and the Virgin's statue, on a small table right next to her daughter's bed.

It is still there now, beside my bed - more than fifty years later.

The cross. It remains with my mum.

A Place Called Home...

The family settled quickly into their new home and soon became familiar with the local area. On most Sundays – when she wasn't working, Bernardete would take her daughter to Mass at the nearby Catholic Church. She soon made many good friends there with whom she would go on to share a lifetime of faith.

The couple were so proud when, at seven years old, Fátima made her First Holy Communion. Bernardete was determined this time, to design and make her daughter's dress for the special occasion.

Stitching strips of white lace onto the pure white fabric, she was reminded of that Christmas Eve all those years ago, when she could not even offer her little girl a christening gown – just a new pink cardigan.

"Thank you God," she whispered, as this sad memory passed and now, with gladness in her heart, she proudly held up the finished garment for Fátima, who was standing in front of her, waiting excitedly to try it on.

As time went on, Bernardete learnt to drive and so Paul bought her a car, enabling her some independence whenever he was at work. She became a confident driver and with her daughter, proudly covered the little Austin MG with stickers of Disney characters – as was fashionable to do in the 70s! Fátima loved going out in that car!

The couple were immensely proud of their young child who had settled in well in her new primary school and had made lots of friends.

It was clear that she had a passion for drawing - often spending hours working on a card or illustrating a story that she had written herself. By the time she was nine years old, she had been entered by her school for a Borough-wide Easter card competition - and had won both first and second prize with her two entries! She had clearly inherited her mother's creative gene.

Meanwhile, Bernardete continued to sew in her own spare time – busily making outfits for herself and her family. She needed no patterns, creating bespoke designs and stitching them together on the sewing machine she had so diligently saved for, all those years ago. Her outfits were greatly admired - friends and family often came to her whenever they needed something made or altered.

As well as sewing, Bernardete continued with her love of learning, keeping an English dictionary and copying down words which she wanted a better understanding of. Drawing upon her own experiences and her faith for inspiration, she would often sit - writing poems and stories. All of these, she then hid away in a small drawer, too shy to reveal them to anyone else.

Only several years later - at her daughter's insistence, did she finally take them out and showed them to her. Fátima had wept as she read these beautiful compositions – stories expressing pain, love and sorrow – many dedicated to those she knew and loved – and also those she had lost.

In one of these poems, she had written about her own mother – of her sadness as each of her children had left her, one after the other. It had referred to each individual in turn and reading it, Fátima could truly imagine the heartache that her poor grandmother must have felt.

Touched and impressed by her writing, she offered to help her mum translate the poem from her native Portuguese into English. Bernardete had objected at first – she did not believe that it would appeal to anyone else but after some persuasion from her confident daughter, she finally relented.

One day as she was glancing through a magazine, Fátima noticed an advert inviting entries to a poetry competition, and excited, she encouraged her mother to enter. To her own surprise and secret delight, Bernardete was awarded a runners up prize and the poem was published! With a collection of others, it was printed in a special edition leather bound book - of which she received a copy to keep for herself.

Fátima was so proud of her, telling everyone of her mother's achievement, and Bernardete - although secretly delighted, showed the book to her husband before she discreetly placed it away in the same little drawer as the others.

She was like that. Always humble.

At home, Bernardete strived to ensure that her daughter grew up disciplined and hardworking. Together, they would clean the whole house every Saturday and only then, would Fátima be permitted to watch television. From an early age, she knew how to iron and also had a basic understanding of how to cook. Each Sunday she would wake her parents with tea and cake – which she had baked herself the night before.

By the time Fátima was ten years old, Paul and Bernardete had sold the house to move to a bigger property, just a short distance away. This garden was massive and badly overrun, neglected by the previous owner. Soon, with the help of their extended family, they soon managed to get it neat and tidy and Fátima spent many happy hours there where she would play with friends and her cousins. In the summer, Paul would barbecue for the relatives as they sat reminiscing and enjoying the sunshine.

Sometimes, on the spur of the moment, one sister would ring the others and they would gather everyone in a convoy of cars and head off to Windsor or Reading, for an impromptu picnic. Between them, they brought chicken, potatoes, rice and salads and drinks – whatever they had at home! If they had no food prepared, this reunion would change to either the nearest motorway service station or Heathrow Airport. There, the adults would sit drinking coffee as their children ran around together.

On one occasion whilst looking for a suitable picnic spot, Fátima's aunt had slipped and fallen - abruptly letting go of the basket of food she was carrying. A whole roast chicken proceeded to roll down the hill, hotly pursued by her uncle who - in his haste to retrieve the escaping chicken, did not even stop to check on his horrified wife!

How everyone had laughed at his reaction, often referring back to this hilarious scene as they reminisced together many years later!

It was a simple time. Yet these precious moments would live on in the memories of the children, even as they grew up.

In their new home, the couple soon discovered a shared enjoyment for growing plants and vegetables. Passers-by often remarked on the beautiful array of flowers, ever-present in the front garden.

Between them, they created a little piece of their individual homelands – Paul with tropical ferns, vines and sweetcorn to remind him of Dominica and Bernardete with potatoes, beans and cabbages – a taste of Madeira. Trees were planted and they grew apples, pears, plums and cherries, cultivating and reaping their crops - which would then be shared with family, friends and neighbours.

When Fátima was twelve years old, Bernardete went back home to Madeira for the first time since she had left back in 1964. The joy in returning to her mother's house and seeing her again, was overwhelming.

Not a lot had changed on this small island and she quickly re-accustomed herself with the places she had previously known so well. Proudly she introduced her husband and daughter to the rest of her family – another brother, aunts, uncles and even more cousins for Fátima!

They had a wonderful three weeks holiday and returned home to England with a passion to return, again and again.

Around the same time, Maria had been contemplating whether, she too should move to London. She realised that she was missing out on seeing most of her grandchildren grow up and knew that in time, she would need some support herself. In the meantime, she would be able to help look after the littler ones whilst their parents worked.

Although she was reluctant to leave the two sons who were still living in Madeira, they both assured her that she had their blessing - if she really wanted to leave.

Her family in England were delighted when - just a year after Bernardete's visit, Maria joined them for good.

A Mother's Dream...

Time passed. Fátima had grown up watching her dad at work in his garage and now aged seventeen, she could not wait to learn to drive herself. She took a Saturday job to pay for lessons and subsequently passed her driving test - first time. Paul was proud of her and secretly relieved. He had always been concerned for her safety and wellbeing and was pleased that she would no longer have to rely on public transport to get around.

The very next evening, he arrived home with a second-hand Ford Escort – a gift for his excited daughter.

Bernardete watched his face light up as Fátima thanked him, clearly overjoyed with her generous surprise.

Silently, she asked God to always bless him – she truly believed he had been a guardian angel in their lives. How very different things might have been, if not for Paul. She truly loved him – they both did.

By now, the young girl had finished school. Having successfully passed all her exams, she discussed with her parents what she wanted to do next.

Paul and Bernardete had always encouraged their daughter to fulfil her ambitions, so they were delighted when she decided to pursue her interest in art. She enrolled at a local college and within two years, completed her studies, graduating with a diploma in General Art and Design.

Keen to take her education further, she had hoped to specialise in animation but was disappointed to discover that, there were no courses on the subject in London. She realised that she would have to apply further afield and was pleased - but nervous, when she was offered a place at Sheffield University.

Bernardete was dismayed – for the first time in her life, she was to be separated from her child.

The day of Fátima's departure to Sheffield arrived far too soon. As they left their daughter behind - so far from home, Paul tried his best to reassure his wife as she sat in the car weeping - for almost the whole three hour journey back.

Fátima suddenly found herself alone in a small cold bedsit - up high in the attic of a stranger's house. And she cried too.

Bernardete prayed for her daughter – so far away. Would she be led astray? What if something happened to her? She recalled her own past - she had been so easily misled and wondered, how her sheltered daughter would cope by herself - away from those who had loved and protected her up until now. Once again, she had to leave her in God's hands.

In Sheffield meanwhile, her daughter was quickly regretting her decision to leave home. Being away from her family was an awakening and Fátima soon realised how much they had always done for her.

She guiltily wondered if she had ever really shown her appreciation...

Bernardete had no need to worry. Realising the sacrifices they had made for her, Fátima was determined not to let her parents down. She would not be like many of her peers who took full advantage of their freedom and the student lifestyle.

Although she made several good friends in Sheffield, Fátima had no inclination to waste her time and money on drinking and going out and - with just a few exceptions, turned down most offers to socialise after college.

Because she was an only child, she actually liked her own company and didn't mind staying indoors. She would spend the time catching up on college work and reading or writing letters home.

She knew that her parents had placed their trust in her and so she was determined that she would do *nothing* to disappoint them.

But deep down, Fátima really missed home. Although Bernardete and Paul had reluctantly allowed her the freedom to make her own way, her letters to them hinted at loneliness - and regret - at her decision to leave.

The course that she had chosen had been stopped suddenly due to lack of funding and Fátima had a lot to think about in determining her future. She did not want to waste precious time on a subject that did not interest her and began to feel very depressed at the situation she had found herself in. Bernardete felt sad for her as she realised that her daughter was confused and all alone – she knew what that felt like.

Paul couldn't stand it. He put in an extra hour's work here and there - and within a few weeks, Fátima was returning home every other weekend, the money for the train ticket transferred into her bank account - by her dad. She would turn up smiling, welcomed every time by her mum who embraced her - as if they hadn't seen each other for years and not just days!

For almost a year, Fátima persevered, but the course was not for her and she decided that she would have to leave. Reluctantly, she told her parents. The change of circumstances were outside of her control, however she still felt guilty that they would not get to see her graduate. She knew it was every parents' dream to experience that special day…

Without hesitation, Paul and Bernardete accepted her decision – they understood that she had tried her best. Ignoring the comments of some who regarded it as a failure, Bernardete defended her daughter - believing it to be as God wished. She trusted Fátima's judgement and had faith that, He would look after her future.

Secretly, she was overjoyed to have Fátima back – her blessed Mother had brought her baby home.

Once back home, Fátima wasted no time in looking for work. Within just a couple of months, she was offered a job as an administrator in central London.

She had also - during that time, met someone special. She was initially worried that her parents might object as she was only twenty years old, but to her relief, Paul and Bernadette were pleased for her. Very soon the young couple were making plans to marry.

Bernardete was happy. She could never have imagined that her life would have been so blessed. As she thought about those early years and all her suffering, the sad memories seemed almost seemed surreal now. Through it all, she had never forgotten the voice she had heard - the promise made from Heaven, that everything would be well.

Bernadette had believed and here was proof that by her faith, she had survived – her beloved daughter, the one who she had refused to give up, now grown and getting married.

She promised to buy Fátima's wedding dress. Sadly, Bernardete now suffered from painful arthritis in her hands and she accepted that this would prevent her from making one herself. She was determined however, to give her daughter the very best that she could – even if it meant working another job in order to pay for it. And that, is exactly what she did.

Bernardete had noticed an advertisement for a cleaner, pinned upon the railings of the house next to her normal place of work. Believing this to be the exactly what she was looking for, she immediately rang the doorbell. It was as if God had seen her necessity and provided the opportunity she needed to achieve her goal. The job was ideal – just two afternoons a week and she could go there straight from her other job.

For a whole year, she worked the extra hours – diligently saving everything she earned.

The time finally came for Fátima to search for the dress for her special day. As in every mother's dream, they shopped for it together – Bernardete's opinion of utmost importance, in her daughter's final choice.

Now, seeing Fátima dressed in white and looking to her for approval, Bernardete could not help but shed a tear – this time, one of happiness.

And on that day, 29th July 1989, her fractured heart was finally mended, as she watched her beloved husband Paul - in his rightful place - walking his daughter down the aisle.

An Ending...

At the end of her memoirs,
my mother wrote down these exact words:

*We are so happy. Time went by so fast – now my baby is
married. Thanks to God for sending us a good man to be my
husband, and father to my daughter.*

*A message to whoever reads my story. Don't give up hope.
When you are sad, turn to God and our own Mother from Heaven
– they will always help you.*
They helped me and I will always be grateful.

Bernardete (The Lonely Heart)

133

The Mum.

My mum was a poet. Not many people knew that she loved to write – she hid her talent. Just one more example of her humility.

I have her poems. Some, she showed me before she died - so moving were they, that we both cried reading them... Others, I found hidden away afterwards. These made me even sadder...

Like the Portuguese Fado[2] which she loved to listen to, they spoke of grief, loss and unrequited love – and were written from her own life experiences. I have tried to translate some of them into English – I cannot do them justice – they need to be in Portuguese.

My mum was devoutly religious, despite her treatment by those nuns – it never diminished her faith. Throughout her life, she still had a great respect for her Church. With a gentle smile for all who met her and a special compassion for those condemned by others – she understood. She was a person who saw the good in everybody and easily forgave the bad.

My precious mum, a truly special soul who loved life – yet always yearned for Heaven. I know she's there.

---

[2] a genre of popular Portuguese song, usually with a melancholy theme

We lost my precious mum, Bernardete on 2 January 2012. She was at home… I am grateful for that blessing.

Three weeks before… Was her birthday. I was glad I could give her a gift that she had always wanted. A statue of St. Faustina – she had always held a special devotion to Jesus of Divine Mercy.

Two weeks before… Was my birthday. She cried because she was bedridden and had nothing to give me. My gift was having her still with me.

One week before… Was Christmas. The priest came. She sang to us and reminded me not to neglect the baby Jesus' birthday - just because she was sick.
She died on her beloved sister's (my Godmother) birthday. Forcing us in her usual selfless way, to celebrate the day – and not to mourn it. That was my mum.

Throughout the most difficult times in her life, my mum's faith never faltered. Her trust in God persevered, as did her belief that everything happened according to His Holy Will.

She accepted it all.

She is loved and missed beyond all words.

The Child.

I am of course, the Child.

My mum told me the truth about where I came from when I was twelve years old. I was shocked but promised myself that I didn't want to know anything about my biological father – he didn't deserve my interest.

Once, curiosity got the better of me and I asked what he had looked like…

She told me to look in the mirror.

I was scared that my face must remind her of the pain he had caused her but I was wrong. My mum loved me before I was born and saw only me – the daughter she had fought for. I feel no resentment towards him – he played his part in my existence - that is it.

All I am is because of the man who raised me.

My dad - who did not hesitate to nurture and love this little girl with no doubt in his heart, that she would be his daughter. My dad - who worked, sacrificed and struggled for the two of us. My dad - who withstood discrimination and doubt to stand by my mum's side - no matter what.

He has supported me in everything, allowing my mistakes and the opportunity to learn from them. His advice has kept me on a straight path – his morals and values always an example, of his integrity.

I pray every day, that I bring him some comfort.

My own story continues... and like my mum, I believe that my faith in God will give me the strength to carry my share... and more.

Dedications:

First and foremost – My dad:
These two small words cannot begin to say what I truly
feel. But I hope you know. *Thank you Dad.*
Love never dies - **We** love you, always.

My immediate family:
For always being there to hold my hand and dry my eyes.
You are everything to me.

My beloved Godparents, cousins and friends who came:
For endless visits, comforting arms and shared tears. *Especially* my
dearest uncle. For feeding us every Sunday for almost a year.
I know the significance of your sacrifice for us.
Every day I ask God, to bless you.

All my family and friends:
For your comfort, support and love – in spite of your own grief.
To the Priests of St. Anselm's Church and Alex from Macmillan – for
your presence whenever we needed you. God bless you always.
And to all who supported my precious mum in those early days -
the ones who held her up and stood by her side in her darkest hours.
Be Blessed – wherever you are.

For those that judged, condemned and doubted – you were wrong.
I forgive you. As she did.

Poetry

composed by Maria Bernardete de Freitas Spínola Paul

Here, I include just two of my mum's poems. These are her very own words, written as they were meant to be read - in the language she first knew - and the one she reverted to at the end...

Canção da Morte

By: Maria Bernardete de Freitas Spínola Paul

1.
Na hora da minha morte
Quero sofrer por autora,
Se alguém estiver com pena
Por favor, se vão embora.

2.
Na hora da minha morte
Não quer que chorem por mim.
Foi Deus que me deu a sorte
E assim será o meu fim.

3.
Adeus querido marido,
Adeus meus irmãos também.
Adeus todos amigos,
Que Deus os ajude em bém.

4.
Adeus querida filha,
Adeus meu genro também.
Adeus querida netinha,
Cuida bém da tua mãe.

5.
Adeus queridos irmãos
E sobrinhos também,
Adeus a toda família
E que Deus os guie em bém.

6.
Não chorem por mim, não chorem
Mais vale pena sorrir,
Que quando chegar ao Céu
Por todos vós vou pedir.

História Verdadeira

By: Maria Bernardete de Freitas Spínola Paul

1.

Foi no mês de Setembro
Quando disse à minha Mãe
Vou até o estrangeiro
Espero que me hei-de dar bem.

2.

A minha querida mãe
Começou logo a chorar
Filha, não penses nisso
Nem nisso deves pensar.

3.

Minha querida mãe
Não esteja a chorar
Que assim que eu posso
Dinheiro lhe ei-de mandar.

4.

Eu sei que somos pobres
Vivemos de dia a dia
Mas eu mais quero aqui, ter
A tua boa companhia.

5.

Só em pensar que podes dar
Com maus companheiras
E nunca mais te lembraras
Da tua mãe verdadeira.

6.

Nisso não deve pensar
Que se eu me der bem
Aqui hei-de voltar
Ver a minha querida mãe.

7.

25 anos tinha
Quando vim para Inglaterra
Muitos lágrimas chorei
Em lembrar-me da minha terra.

8.

Nem só da minha terra
Mas dos meus irmãos também
Ainda mais chorava
Pela minha querida mãe.

9.
Assim passavam os dias
Meses e anos também
Passava mais animada
Com as cartas da minha mãe.

10.
Quando dois anos passava
Sozinha a passear
Quando me pergunta um homem
Porque è que estava a chorar.

11.
As lágrimas eram tantos
Que não consegui falar
Quando me diz aquele homem
Vamos um café tomar.

12.
Ele com boas palavras
Conseguia-me animar
Nunca pensando eu
Que me ia falsear.

13.
Quando passava algumas meses
Aquele falso rapaz
Tanto me prometia
Que pensava ser de mais.

14.
Quando um dia percebi
Que não me sentia bem
Pois nunca me pensava
Que la ia eu ser mãe.

15.
Agora que tristeza
O que iria acontecer
Mas quando nisto lhe falei
Ele não quizo saber.

16.
Não sabendo o que fazer
Só pensava era chorar
Então quando resolvi
Irei eu me matar.

17.
Estando eu na plataforma
A espera de me matar
Quando uma linda voz ouvi
Não! Eu ei-de te ajudar.

18.
Olhei para todos os lados
Ali não vendo ninguém
Aquela voz veio do Céu
É a minha querida Mãe.

19.

Então voltei para casa
Muito cheia de alegria
O! Querida Mãe do Céu
Serás a minha companhia.

20.

Até que prometi
Se tudo corrês-se bém
A minha filha daria
O nome da minha Mãe.

21.

Indo um dia para casa
Com tudo isso pensava
Quando ao meu pé para um carro
E um rapaz apitava.

22.

Menina, minha menina
É favor de me informar
Se vai para muito longe
Em meu carro hei-de a levar.

23.

Eu não vou para muito longe
E no seu carro eu não vou
Sr! Deixe-me em paz
Bem vê como è que estou!

24.

Menina não tenha medo
Mal não lhe vou fazer
Apenas a-quero ajudar
Porque a estou a conhecer.

25.

Não me deve conhecer
Isso è de admirar
Eu não vivo nesta ária
Uma irmã vim visitar.

26.

È de ai que a conhêço
Agora me lembro bém
Eu conheço a sua Irmã
E o noivo dela também.

27.

Ate que resolvi
No carro dele eu entrei
Passados algumas meses
Eu com ele namorei.

28.

Assim passavam os dias
Que ele me acompanhava
Sentia-me tão feliz
Nem sequer acreditava.

29.

Até que chegou o dia
Da minha filha nascer
Era uma bela menina
Que até me custou a crer.

30.

Quando pela madrugada
O Paul ali chegou
Paul, vê a minha filha
Ai! que contente eu estou!

31.

Bernardete, Bernardete!
Isto te quero dizer
Quero que se case comigo
O pai dela eu quero ser.

32.

Foi então quando pensei
Quando me ia matar
Quando aquela voz ouvi
Em que me ia ajudar.

33.

E assim aconteceu
Que grande alegria eu tinha
Foi a 23 de Junho
Ja não vivia sozinha.

34.

Assim passaram os meses
E muitos anos também
Que o meu querido Paul
Não pensava em mais ninguém.

35.

Agora era feliz
Mas muito ainda esperava
O futuro da minha filha
Era o que eu mais pensava.

36.

Agora mais uma vez
Pensava muito também
Só quem a pode ajudar
É a nossa querida Mãe.

37.

Estudava noite e dia
A nossa querida filha
Obrigada Mãe do Céu
Que alegria eu tinha.

38.

Até que chegou o dia
De o seu curso tirar
Quando tinha 20 anos
Começou a namorar.

39.

Namorou um bom rapaz
Melhor não poderia ser
Bem pedi à Mãe do Céu
Para assim acontecer.

40.

No 29 de Julho
Grande dia de alegria
Que a minha filha casou
Obrigado, Virgem Maria.

41.

Rapazes e raparigas
Nunca se esqueçem de mim
Muito triste no principio
Mas muito alegre no fim.

My mum,
Maria Bernardete de Freitas Spínola Paul

Photographs

Top
Bernardete, standing outside her
mother's house in Funchal, taken
prior to leaving Madeira for England

Right
1962. Bernardete, dressed in black,
less than a year after the loss of her
father and grandfather

Above
1963. Bernardete, taken in a
photography studio in Funchal

Above
1965. Bernardete, ready for the
British Winter – taken when she
started working at University
College Hospital, Gower Street

Left
1965. Bernardete, already
pregnant – in the garden
of her residence in
St. John's Wood, with the
couple's little dog

Below
My Mum, Bernardete and Me.

Lightning Source UK Ltd.
Milton Keynes UK
UKHW04f1328200718
326032UK00001B/67/P